MW00639022

BY DESIGN

Developing a Philosophy of Education
Informed by a Christian Worldview

Martha E. MacCullough, EdD

purposeful design®
p u b l i c a t i o n s

Colorado Springs, CO

Purposeful Design Publications is the publishing division of the Association of Christian Schools International (ACSI) and is committed to the ministry of Christian school education, to enable Christian educators and schools worldwide to effectively prepare students for life. As the publisher of textbooks, trade books, and other educational resources within ACSI, Purposeful Design Publications strives to produce biblically sound materials that reflect Christian scholarship and stewardship and that address the identified needs of Christian schools around the world.

The views expressed in this publication are those of the author, and they may not necessarily represent the position of the Association of Christian Schools International.

Unless otherwise identified, all Scripture quotations are taken from the Holy Bible, NEW INTERNATIONAL VERSION®, NIV® Copyright © 1973, 1978, 1984 by Biblica, Inc. All rights reserved worldwide. Used by permission of Biblica, Inc.

Printed in the United States of America

25 24 23 22 21 20 19 18 17   1 2 3 4 5 6 7

MacCullough, Martha Elizabeth.

By design: Developing a philosophy of education informed by a Christian worldview

Second edition

ISBN 978-1-58331-555-2 Catalog #6670

Editing and page layout (first edition): Carolyn Clare Givens

Editorial team (second edition): Marissa A. Rumpf, Chandler Birch

Design team: John Mulvaney, Mike Riester

Purposeful Design Publications

A Division of ACSI

PO Box 65130 • Colorado Springs, CO 80962-5130
Customer Service: 800-367-0798 • www.acsi.org

Leslie Carrillo
661-486-3809
West Coast
Baptist College

In memory of my husband,

Donald, who was the consummate

Christian educator and encourager

and

to our two daughters,

Sheryl and Debbie, both educators in their own right,

whom we cherished and for whom our interest

in Christian education was greatly advanced.

Moralism
Humanism
  relativism
 Empiricism
  Pragmatism

Table of Contents

Foreword

In 2013, Cairn University celebrated its centennial anniversary. The history of the institution is rich. What began as a Bible institute for lay leaders has emerged as a dynamic and growing Christian university committed to the centrality of Christ and His Word. Over the course of its 100 years, the institution has benefitted from the gifts, wisdom, and sacrificial service of men and women who pioneered an approach to higher education that is intentionally and distinctly biblical.

Over the past 30 years, no individuals have had a more lasting or significant impact on the philosophy of education at the university than Doctors Don and Marti MacCullough. Don served as both undergraduate and graduate dean as well as the university's first provost. His legacy of educational excellence and focus on professional practice has shaped much of who we are. His wife, Marti, now Distinguished Professor Emerita, served as chair of the education program and as the school of education's first dean. Marti's thumbprints can be found all over the university and upon countless numbers of teachers in both Christian and public education settings. She set the bar high for biblical integration, championed the cause of worldview-based pedagogy, and shaped the educational philosophy of multiple generations of teachers, including many of us who teach now at Cairn. Dr. Marti MacCullough has served with distinction. She taught us all that to teach well and in a manner that is coherent and wholly integrated takes work. It does not happen by accident.

This book will be used in our classrooms and will no doubt find its way into the curricula of colleges and universities who are committed to preparing Christian teachers for both private and public schools. It will also serve schools that are seeking tools for faculty development regarding worldview integration. It will serve individuals seeking personal growth as teachers in their own professions. We believe this will be a great benefit to the cause in which we educators are engaged. There is a crisis in our schools today, even in our own Christian schools where we espouse biblical integration and Christian worldview. It is not so much that we are not committed to these things. It is not that we do not value them or expect them from our teachers. I believe it is that we simply need to know how to do it well, effectively, and with purpose. Marti is a master at this work of teaching teachers.

As educators, we know that good teaching and transformational learning do not happen on their own. Teachers have the privilege and responsibility to create and to design lesson plans, classroom activities, and evaluation tools. But there must be sound thinking undergirding all of that work. A philosophy of education requires thoughtful effort. When done rightly, it shapes instruction. The same care and effort taken to create and design the educational deliverables in the classroom should be given to the shaping of a philosophy of education. And for the Christian, this cannot be done outside of our faith commitments and our understanding of eternal truths.

I think this very practical book will give others access to what we know here at Cairn: that we all can learn much from the wisdom, experience, and guidance of Dr. Marti MacCullough. Only Dr. Frank Gaebelein has equaled Dr. Marti MacCullough in shaping my own education assumptions regarding worldview and biblical integration. It is our hope and prayer that many will be strengthened in their work as teachers by what is contained in this book.

Todd J. Williams, PhD

President, Cairn University

December 2012

Acknowledgements

In the writing of this book, I am indebted to the teachers who influenced my thinking in my early educational years: Bible and philosophy professors at Cairn University; philosophy and Christian educators at Wheaton College, especially Dr. Lois LeBar; and the hundreds of my students who have taken the philosophy of education course represented in this book. I am also thankful for the teachers and administrators who have been the inspiration to write this book when they would attend seminars on the topic and ask if there was something in writing that they could use related to the content and format of the sessions. This, in part, is the answer to their inquiry.

I acknowledge and appreciate the incredible support from the Cairn University administration in the decision to publish the first edition of this book. The encouragement of President Dr. Todd Williams has been an undergirding support any faculty member would accept with deep appreciation, and I am grateful. His own developed philosophy of education, informed by a biblical worldview and fleshed out in his presidency and thus in the curriculum of the university, has been encouraging evidence that understanding all of life and learning from God's perspective can be pursued in higher education.

For the faculty in the school of education at the university, who worked alongside their dean in the fleshing out of a philosophy of education informed by a biblical worldview, I am thankful and owe a debt of gratitude. Their effort to live out our vision of the integral relationship between our Christian worldview and education, while appreciated so much by me, is well documented and appreciated by their many students who have graduated and gone on to become educators who are biblically minded and professionally competent, the most important goal of the content of this book.

I acknowledge and appreciate the former president of Cairn University, Dr. Sherrill Babb, who hired my late husband and me and allowed us to work together toward establishing a strong school of education that educated teachers for service to students in private, public, Christian, and international schools under the abiding philosophy of education that is informed by a Christian view of the human and learning.

The untiring work of those who have edited this book for the first and second editions, along with those who have contributed to the layout and book cover, is much appreciated. The book would not have come to fruition without their work.

Finally, I acknowledge and appreciate my daughter educators, Sheryl and Debbie, for whom my early desire for education that is carried out by those who think and act biblically was spurred onward. Both are educators. I love and appreciate both of them and I am delighted that they are Christian women working in the field of education and living out a philosophy of education informed by a Christian worldview.

I would be remiss if I did not mention that all of the content of this book was developed and discussed over many, many years with my loving husband, Don, who went home to be with the Lord before he could read what he had been encouraging me to write for many years. Our love deepened as we spent many hours discussing Christian education, a focus of our hearts and lifelong ministry. Most of all, I am thankful to the Lord for those years of ministry together and for His work in our lives and in the field of Christian education.

Marti MacCullough, EdD

Distinguished Professor Emerita, Cairn University

Introduction

The purpose of this book is to help Christian educators or soon-to-be educators working in Christian schools, other private schools, charter schools, international schools, cyber schools, public schools, or home schools, to intentionally develop a personal philosophy of education informed by a Christian perspective on life and learning. The document derived from the exercise of writing one's philosophy will serve as a guide for developing and evaluating educational practices that are consistent with a Christian worldview, the integrating core for thinking and acting as a biblically minded and professionally competent educator.

The title of this book, *By Design*, designates the process of developing a philosophy of education informed by a Christian worldview as deliberate and intentional, rather than accidental and haphazard. The title carries a double meaning; first, that the Christian worldview is the perspective of the designer of the universe, and second, that the process of developing one's philosophy of education is completed by a designer, the person doing the thinking and crafting, using a pattern or plan such as the one suggested in this book. Lastly, the use of the term *design* in the title follows the Merriam-Webster definition: "to devise for a specific function or end." That end is to carry out one's ministry and service in a way that honors the Designer and is informed by a coherent view of life and learning.

On the one hand, this book includes textbook-type general knowledge to stimulate thinking on the part of the reader; on the other hand, it is designed much like a workbook. However, it is not intended to be either. The nature of this book is interactive by design. Some sections provide more content than others when it was determined that there was a need for an overview of current thinking and practices.

Readers are encouraged to stop, reflect, and write as they use the cues and prompts provided by the author. The intent of the author is to guide the reader in the writing of a philosophy of education document.

The activities found throughout the book are designed to assist readers in the process of examining and systematizing their thoughts. There are several kinds of activities included in the text: read to find out, research, think, write, discuss with others, and combinations of those five.

Section One introduces the concept of an educational philosophy and a typical process one follows in developing a personal working philosophy of education. In this section, key terms are defined, reflection on current beliefs of the reader is guided by questions and activities, the connection between a general philosophy of life or worldview and one's educational philosophy is addressed, and the development and writing of the aim of education is explored.

Section Two introduces the key elements of an educational philosophy, the nature of the student and learning, the role of the teacher in the learning event, and the nature and purpose of the curriculum.

Section One Introduction

> "Christianity, if false, is of no importance, and, if true, of infinite importance. The one thing it cannot be is moderately important."
>
> —C. S. Lewis, *Christian Apologetics*, p. 101

Why write a book that guides Christian educators toward a distinctively Christian educational philosophy? Is it necessary to bring one's specific worldview to the process of learning and the resulting implications for education? C. S. Lewis provided a good answer to that question many years ago when he spoke at a conference for Anglican ministers and youth leaders in Wales. His words have often been cited and are recorded in his book *God of the Docks,* but were first published under the essay title "Christian Apologetics." There is no place for biblical Christianity to be moderately important! If Christianity is true, it is of infinite importance, and there can be no endeavor that resides outside of that framework. Therefore, serious Christian educators will make sure that their personal philosophies of education are informed by a Christian worldview. ✓

• Whatever your philosophy is one must be able to defend it.

eg/ Christian faith

An Educational philosophy must be centered on the principles of God's word

1 | What Is a Philosophy of Education?

[handwritten annotation: viewpoint = I have made this belief my own*]*

All students, teachers, and administrators have a viewpoint about education. Their views have been developed over years of being a student, participating in informal teaching venues, or teaching and serving in schools. Some began adopting their professional views about education while enrolled in schools of education, programs of certification, and clinical teaching experiences. Some are currently college or university students still in that process of developing and shaping their views.

The point is that we all have a viewpoint about what makes for "good" educational practices. The difference between these "viewpoints" related to education and a *philosophy of education* is not so much a difference in what we ultimately come to believe, but rather whether or not those "beliefs" have been examined, systematized, and intentionally accepted as one's own. Before intentionally developing a *personal* philosophy of education, some of our beliefs may be borrowed from professors who have taught us, textbooks and other educational media we have read or seen, or from the latest educational journal, educational book espousing a new innovation, or current "best practices" addressed in a professional development seminar. These beliefs may not have been examined and internalized by the student or teacher. Some beliefs are held consistently; others are not. A disciplined exercise in developing a personal philosophy of education begins with a current educational viewpoint and proceeds to clarify, adapt, confirm, or change beliefs in order to develop an internally consistent and coherent educational philosophy (one that makes sense and sticks together as a whole) that is informed by one's worldview.

This book will help educators or prospective educators to intentionally reflect upon their current beliefs in light of a Christian worldview. A worldview provides answers to the major questions of life. In the case of education, these are questions that directly relate to the nature of the human being and learning, the role of a leader/teacher and teaching, the nature of knowledge and knowing, and the aim of life that informs the aim of the school curriculum and education as a whole.

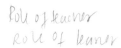
[handwritten annotation: Role of teacher / Role of learner*]*

Defining the Term: Philosophy of Education

For a period of time in the mid-twentieth century, an approach to doing philosophy called "analytic philosophy" became more popular among educators than classical or traditional philosophy (the approach taken in this book). Analytic philosophy is based upon a naturalistic worldview that accepts as truth only that which can be discovered or uncovered with the senses. This analytic approach categorizes worldview metanarratives that are based upon a starting point other than nature or the natural world as "non-sense." Thus, most would have little interest in a Christian worldview.

While analytic philosophers do not personally appreciate a worldview approach to philosophy, they have contributed something to our endeavor. Analytic philosophy is primarily linguistic analysis. As such, it has contributed to the ongoing conversation in philosophy by requiring disciplines such as education to more carefully define and clarify the language they use to communicate. This has been a positive contribution to the classical (or traditional) approach to philosophy, which we are taking in this book.

In *Philosophy and Education: An Introduction in Christian Perspective* (2006), George Knight described the classic approach this way:

> The function of educational philosophy has traditionally been to develop and prescribe aims and practices that are built upon and are in harmony with a philosophic outlook based on a particular view concerning the nature of reality, truth, and value (pp. 150–151).

In the early 1980s, I took a course in my doctoral program called *Analytic Philosophy of Education*. For four hours a day, three days a week, for four weeks, we analyzed phrases such as, "education that...," "education to...," and "education for..." Educational mantras of the day were also analyzed. One such mantra was, "Education is life, rather than preparation for life." Each word in the sentence and the grammatical structure of the statements were examined and analyzed. My contribution to the class interaction was offering a statement for analysis that is often said of parents who send their children to Christian or parochial schools: that these parents are "sheltering their kids from the real world." Fellow classmates— teachers and administrators from private schools and the nuns and priests who were parochial school educators—enjoyed the analysis, for they had heard the same thing and wondered how those who held that view defined the "real world." To the thinking of private school educators, schools (even private schools) are part of the

Philosophy reflects my view of reality, truth, value

real world. While I must admit that much of the course was tedious and at times boring, I learned the importance of defining terms in order to communicate more clearly. I have found it important to begin the journey of developing a Christian philosophy of education by defining and describing the terms *philosophy* and *education.*

[handwritten: Define terms in order communicate more clearly.]

Activity | What Do You Think?

In the course I teach at the university, this is where we begin.

Take a minute to write all of the descriptors that come to your mind when you think of the word *philosophy*. List these under the word or create a concept map with *philosophy* as the key word.

Philosophy

[handwritten notes:]
- belief
- values
- principles
- practice
- point of view
- teaching methods
- cause
- effect
- reasonings
- knowledge
- perspective
- principles
- values
- thought process
- concepts
- reason

After you have done the above, add the words *of education* to the word *philosophy* and do the same thing. List descriptors that come to mind when you think about the term *philosophy of education.*

Philosophy of Education

[handwritten notes:]
- imparting of knowledge
- teaching and training
- Imparting of truth
- building knowledge
- reasons to educate
- ideas/models implemented
- right way to teach
- teaching methods.

- Comparing your two lists, write a statement that reflects the similarities, differences, and perhaps the relationship (as you see it now) between a philosophy (as in a general philosophy of life) and a philosophy of education.

[handwritten in margin: why, how, when]

[handwritten: what purpose of it. Philosophy and education go hand in hand you cannot have one without the other. know when which why common standard in everything education takes place]

Here are examples from the list produced by one of my philosophy of education classes. If you did not create your own list, use these to draw conclusions related to similarities, differences, and relationships. What is one obvious difference between the two? How might the two sets be related?

Philosophy	Philosophy of Education
• Logic	• Value of education
• Enlightenment	• What is worth knowing?
• Socrates	• Purpose or aim of education
• Plato	• Who is qualified to teach?
• Aristotle	• Environment and classroom management
• Love of wisdom	• Christian vs. secular, private vs. public
• Curious	• Individual learning
• Beliefs	• Nature of human beings
• Why?	• Worldview questions and curriculum
• Academics	
• Understanding	
• Questions	
• Higher order thinking	
• Knowledge	
• Deep thinking	

philosophy view concerning the nature of reality truth and value.

value rather than just why.

personal philosophy: views held that are the results of personal study and examination.

actions → based on principles God has solidify in your heart.

wisdom:

Defining the Term: *Philosophy*

The definition of the word *philosophy* may be found in any dictionary. Coming from the Greek Φιλοσοφία (philosophia), the word literally means "love of wisdom" (philo—love, sophia—wisdom).

When educators are serious about their discipline, how they perceive their learners, and the knowledge to which they expose their learners, they will "love wisdom" in their tasks as educators. Therefore, every educator should want to develop an intentionally held philosophy of education. *Educato: love wisdom*

A general philosophy of life is a set of beliefs that answers life's biggest questions related to reality (existence), knowing, and values (including conduct), that has been examined and intentionally accepted by a group, person, or faith tradition. These issues (questions) are basically the subdivisions of philosophy: metaphysics, epistemology, and axiology. This is a simple definition; however, it is worthwhile to research definitions of philosophy that are promoted in the discipline (education) by philosophers from various perspectives.

It is also helpful to study definitions for *wisdom*. From a Christian perspective, one thing is clear: the beginning of wisdom is the fear of the Lord. The starting *Prov 9:10* point for wisdom is the God of the universe. Therefore, the foundational belief in a Christian philosophy is a statement about God and the kind of God He is. Christians begin with God, rather than humans or nature, in the expression of their philosophies of life. *wisdom: knowledge applied.*

Writing a Philosophy of Education

A philosophy of education is a set of beliefs that has been intentionally examined and accepted as a framework out of which to develop a view of (1) the aim of education, (2) the nature of the student and learning, (3) the role of the teacher and teaching, and (4) the nature and purpose of the curriculum. These four beliefs will impact the thinking and acting of an educator. These fundamental elements form the framework for a philosophy of education, a type of manifesto or public declaration of beliefs in document format with little or no illustrations, redundancy, or fluff. In the past, my students were asked to write a 10–20 page document; however, in the last 15 years or so, that requirement has been changed to a three-to-five page statement of educational beliefs. A shorter version actually requires far more reflection, integration, and organization than the longer version.

beliefs · aim — roles student — teacher — Nature view and and & learning teaching purpose of curriculum.

Relationship Between a General Philosophy and a Philosophy of Education

All philosophies of education come from somewhere. Educational philosophies are informed by underlying "root" or general philosophical beliefs. There is indeed a relationship between one's philosophy of education and one's general philosophy of life or worldview. I am not using the last two terms interchangeably but am aware that, while everyone has a worldview, not everyone has an examined and systematized philosophy of life. So, where do we begin? We will use the terms "Christian worldview" or "biblical worldview" to describe our roots rather than using the term "general philosophy," which usually refers to fully developed philosophies such as Idealism, Realism, Neo-Scholasticism, Pragmatism, Existentialism, and (to some extent) Postmodernism and Neo-Marxism. That said, it is still worthwhile to study the leading general philosophies. These form the roots for modern-day philosophies of education.

> "Education must share with religion or philosophy its perspective on the world at large and the human being's place in this world…. Education as such possesses no substance of itself…. Education is the instrument for carrying out society's philosophical goals." *"imparting of knowledge will carrying out God's will/plan"*
>
> —D. Bruce Lockerbie, *Who Educates Your Child?* p. 46

Activity   Suggested Research

This study can be done on your own, with a group, or in a class.

A good exploration is to take the leading modern philosophies of education that have been developed and are in current use by educators worldwide and trace their underlying root (general) philosophies—that is, the major underlying philosophical beliefs that inform the specific educational philosophy and practices.

Some of these modern educational philosophies are:

- Behaviorism
- Essentialism or Neo-Essentialism
- Perennialism
- Educational Humanism
- Futurism

- Progressivism
- Educational Anarchism (Deschooling)
- Reconstructionism (which may broadly include Critical Pedagogy, Feminism, Globalism, Multiculturalism and other current "isms")

Students in my course read and chart these using Philosophy and Education: An Introduction in Christian Perspective by George Knight. This text, now in its fourth edition, has been used for many years as a good summary of general and educational philosophies. Almost any philosophy of education textbook, however, will include some or most of the educational philosophies listed above and will also briefly address the underlying root philosophies: Idealism, Realism, Pragmatism, and Existentialism. Some include Neo-Scholasticism, Marxism, and Postmodernism as well. An educator's study should include an exploration of the beliefs about the student, the teacher, and the curriculum held by the eight or so modern philosophies of education. These philosophies of education have grown out of or been derived from one of the major general philosophies.

How Teachers Think and Talk About Philosophy of Education

Rather than converse with colleagues or fellow students using the five general root philosophies or the eight or so modern educational philosophies, most teachers just claim to be either "traditional" or "progressive" in their philosophy of education. These pop educational labels are still used in educational journal articles today and by teachers as they converse in the teacher's lounge and faculty meetings—whether or not the beliefs inherent in the labels have been examined, systematized, or clarified. I have found that when most educators discuss these two pop labels they are thinking more of methodology than a comprehensive set of beliefs. *well-thought - digested beliefs that will produce bring fruit*

Note: An in-depth study of general philosophies and modern philosophies of education informed by these general philosophies is beyond the scope of this book. However, it should be a part of the study of the serious student who wishes not only to develop his or her own personal philosophy of education informed by a Christian worldview, but also to know the tenets of each of the other views in order to identify agreement and disagreement. This provides a much broader and more robust approach and opens communication lines with other educators.

Activity Reflect—Traditional or Progressive?

It might be productive to stop here and answer this hypothetical question that might be posed in an interview by an administrator or hiring committee. The administrator asks:

"Do you consider yourself to be *traditional* or more *progressive* in your philosophy of education, and why?" *Traditional: believe in the authority of God's word*

What would you say? How might you answer a colleague or fellow student who asked you that question? Commit to either *traditional* or *progressive* and then write one belief that you hold tenaciously that you think might fit under that category or label. This will help you acknowledge prior beliefs that will be examined as you take this journey in developing your own philosophy of education. Below is an exercise that might begin to create disequilibrium that will help you to deliberately evaluate your current beliefs.

Activity | Inventory of Beliefs

The following inventory is typical of those printed in foundations of education and pedagogy textbooks for pre-service teachers. Try your hand. Read the directions carefully!

Your Current Beliefs About Education

Mark an "X" between the dots (not on the dots) on the continuum in the direction in which you most closely lean.

1. Do you believe that the most important purpose of education is to help children acquire content knowledge, facts, principles, and basic skills in reading, writing, and arithmetic (e.g., products of education), or to help children learn how to learn, solve problems, and think creatively (e.g., the processes of education)?

    Products of Education : X :___:___:___: *Processes of Education*

2. Do you believe that the basic role of the teacher is that of being a dispenser of knowledge and information or that of facilitating children's own knowledge constructions?

    Dispenser of Knowledge : X :___:___:___: *Facilitator of Personal Knowledge*

3. Do you believe that the student's role should be that of a passive receptor in the learning process or that of an active participant in the personal learning process?

    Passive Receptor :___:___:___: X : *Active Participant*

4. Do you believe that knowledge remembered (facts, concepts, principles) should be the focus of learning or knowledge for action and use?

    Remembered :___:___:___: X : *Basis of Action*

5. Do you believe that knowledge is still being accumulated, varies from time to time, and is open to various interpretations; or do you believe most knowledge has been accumulated, is unchangeable, and is only open to specific interpretation?

    Emerging and Varying :___:___:___: X : *Emerged and Unchangeable*

6. Do you believe that truth is absolute and objective or relative and subjective?

    Absolute and Objective : X :___:___:___: *Relative and Subjective*

7. Do you believe that children learn from within (by internal structuring of experiences and ideas into new ideas created by the learner) or from without (by external structuring of the learning event and correct rewarding of the learner's responses by a teacher)?

Learn from Within :___:___:___:X: Learn from Without *what childrens need within — Be in middle*

8. Do you believe that people are basically evil (tend toward making wrong choices) or basically good (tend toward honesty and right choices)?

Basically Evil :___X___:___:___: Basically Good

With which questions above did you have the most problem with, and why? This is a good activity to discuss with a colleague. Another challenge is to write a T or a P (for traditional or progressive) at the end of each pole of the continuum and discuss why you labeled as you did. Compare your own chosen label, "Traditional" or "Progressive" with the choices you made on this exercise. What conclusion can you draw about your own beliefs? Write it here:

Traditional | progressive
teacher | student
teacher | creativity
impart of | explore
knowl

Reading About Other Philosophies of Education and Their Roots

One of the major reasons I require a reading and summary of modern educational philosophies and their underlying general philosophies is to clearly show how educational philosophy is not something you develop by eclectically choosing whatever is popular at the moment, the fad or innovation of the day, or what is easiest to do in practice. Nor is it something that should be inconsistent with your view of life. Christian educators should begin to see that just as those who come from other worldviews have a starting point, so too, must they. Underlying worldview beliefs will form the foundation or integrating core for their educational beliefs and practices if indeed they are consistent, coherent, integrated, and intentional.

This idea that beliefs related to the aim of education are necessarily related to one's aim of life was reinforced by Robert Rusk in his landmark book, *The Philosophical Bases of Education* (1956). He wrote:

> The answer to every educational question is ultimately influenced by our philosophy of life. Although few formulate it, every system of education must have an aim and the aim of education is relative to the aim of life. Philosophy formulates what it conceives to be the end [the aim] of life; education offers suggestions how this end is to be achieved (p. 15).

· philosophy = aim of life
education = hours end to
be achieved

2 | Using a Worldview Approach to Develop a Philosophy of Education

Understanding *Worldview*

If there is indeed a close connection between one's philosophy of life or worldview and one's philosophy of education, the logical place to begin is by describing briefly one's root beliefs: your Christian beliefs related to the major questions of life. One could use the issues in philosophy: reality/existence, knowing and knowledge, and values related to the good and beautiful. Or one could begin with a series of questions that generally fall under those philosophical categories but are more often called worldview questions. I choose to use the latter approach because most educators have not taken many, if any, courses in philosophy nor have they conducted the disciplined study of the historically full-blown general philosophies that might be necessary for the first approach. However, all educators do have a worldview.

Dutch theologian Albert Wolters, describing the roots of the concept of worldview, explains it this way:

> Whatever its semantic history, the term "worldview" (or its equivalent "world-and-life view") seems to pinpoint a useful distinction between philosophy as a methodologically rigorous academic discipline (a "science" in the sense of *Wissenschaft*), and the commonsense perspective on life and the world, the "system of values" or "ideology," which in one form or another is held by all normal adult human beings regardless of intelligence or education. In this sense, worldview does indeed precede science, and is therefore quite different from philosophy in the strictly theoretical sense (as cited in Hart, van der Hoeven, and Wolterstorff 1983, p. 114).

Wolters goes on to say . . .

> For Christian philosophers, the obvious implication is that they must seek to orient their philosophizing to a Christian worldview. Or to put the case a bit more strongly and accurately, the Christian must seek to philosophize on the basis of the Christian worldview—that is, the biblical worldview (p. 115).

Organizational Structure for Framing a Worldview

Since the mid-1970s, I have used the seven or eight worldview questions found in the book *The Universe Next Door: A Basic Worldview Catalog* by James Sire. Whatever you choose to use to help with the philosophical framework, simply write your general beliefs as a preamble or opening declaration of the underlying worldview that you espouse. If you have taken several philosophy courses and studied in depth the full-blown major philosophies of Idealism, Realism, Neo-Scholasticism or Neo-Thomism, Pragmatism, Existentialism, or Postmodernism, you may wish to see which of these is best suited to your beliefs as a Christian and simply do as some scholars have done: assert that you are a Christian Idealist, or Christian Realist, or Christian whatever.

I prefer to use a worldview framework. Worldview questions are questions stemming from each of the major issues in philosophy. In fact, philosophy is all about asking and trying to answer questions. Using a questions-based approach is one way to develop and declare your "roots." Here are some examples of questions that fit the basic philosophical categories you might use in writing your foundational beliefs in the opening of your philosophy of education document.

Metaphysics (Questions related to existence)—What is ultimate reality? Why is there something rather than nothing? Does God exist? What kind of God is He? If God exists, what role does He play in human affairs? What is a human being, and what is his nature and destiny? What is the nature of the external world, the universe?

Reality in general: Metaphysics.

Epistemology (Questions related to knowing)—How do we know? Why do we know something rather than nothing? Is knowledge subjective or objective, relative or absolute, discovered or created, or what? What are the nature, sources, and validity of knowledge?

"prove"

opinion based on / facts

knowledge "is it objective you can prove it." created a lie?

eg/ Bible ethics.

Axiology (Questions related to value)—What is of value? What are right values and right actions? How do we determine right and wrong, the good and the beautiful?

Ethics, Absolute truth.

Different underlying philosophies answer differently the questions stemming from each of these philosophical categories. For example, below are some possible answers to these questions.

worldviews: can be so different.

Naturalism/Materialism

Issues related to **existence** *= metaphysics*	• Ultimate reality is matter • Humans are material only *(humans are created in God's image)* • There is no spiritual or nonmaterial part of humans • There is no life after physical death—just decomposing matter
Issues related to **knowing**	• Humans know truth through their senses only *=* • The method of truth judging is empirical
Issues related to **valuing** *(morals)*	• Values are "born out of the human experiment" • Values are open to public/group consensus (what works in the experiment of life)

Pantheism / Eastern Mysticism

Issues related to **existence**	• Ultimate reality is impersonal energy • Humans are a part of that energy • Humans are "sleeping gods" • There is life after death—reincarnation • The goal is to become one with the eternal impersonal force
Issues related to **knowing**	• Humans know truth through personal experience or enlightenment • Humans find their own truth • The method for truth-judging is personal and individual
Issues related to **valuing**	• Values are what we decide as individuals • Turn inward—trust your heart! • Values are private and personal, not public

Most Christians would not address these issues as they are addressed above. When we ask, for example, "What is ultimate reality?" the Christian Theistic view would be, "God is." But this is not an impersonal-energy-force-god, nor a god created by the human brain to satisfy some biological or psychological evolutionary need. Our God is a transcendent creator and yet a personal God: a sovereign, just, holy, and loving God; One who reveals Himself to humans in His world (all of His created order), in His Word, and in His Son. He is the God of the Bible.

Armand Nicholi, Harvard University professor of psychology, teaches a course that addresses the vast differences between the worldviews of two notable men, Sigmund Freud, a naturalist and atheist all of his life, and C. S. Lewis, an atheist who was converted to Christianity in his mid-thirties. Nicholi's book *The Question of God* (2002) describes much of his course. He affirms the importance of one's worldview. In it he says,

> Our worldview informs our personal, social, and political lives. It influences how we perceive ourselves, how we relate to others, how we adjust to adversity, and what we understand to be our purpose. Our worldview helps to determine our values, our ethics, and our capacity for happiness. It helps us understand where we come from, our heritage; who we are, our identity; why we exist on this planet, our purpose; what drives us, our motivation; and where we are going, our destiny (p. 7).

In addressing the two vastly different worldviews represented by Freud and Lewis, Nicholi covers many of the issues above and asks, "Can they both be true?"

> Are these worldviews merely philosophical speculations with no right or wrong answer? No. One of them begins with the basic premise that God does not exist, the other with the premise that He does. They are, therefore, mutually exclusive—if one is right the other must be wrong (p. 8).

Our beliefs matter! In developing a philosophy of education, our underlying answers to life's biggest questions are foundational.

A Worldview Approach

In getting started, I suggest that you use a worldview approach that answers the big questions of life and do this from a broad Christian Theistic perspective. Your Christian worldview will form the integrating core for your educational beliefs and will inform and support your developing educational philosophy.

You may have begun this journey toward developing an educational philosophy as one who has never taken a course in philosophy, as is the case of so many of my graduate students. Or you may have had some background in philosophy or theology as most of my undergraduate students do. Choose the framework that fits your background best and use the issues in philosophy (metaphysics, epistemology, and axiology) or the questions below that frame a worldview. There is no need at this time to address the "family squabbles" that have occurred among those who adhere to a Christian worldview, such as mode of baptism or form of church governance. Rather, it is useful to use the broad biblical beliefs of historical Christianity. You will see in the questions below that specific denominational distinctions, although very important, are not always addressed in a broad Christian Theistic worldview.

Here are the questions James Sire uses in his book *The Universe Next Door* (2009, pp. 22–23).

1. What is prime reality—the really real (ultimate or starting reality)?
2. What is the nature of external reality, that is, the world around us?
3. What is a human being?
4. What happens to a person at death?
5. Why is it possible to know anything at all?
6. How do we know what is right and wrong?
7. What is the meaning of human history?
8. What personal life-orienting core commitments (that is, life implications) are consistent with this worldview?

Activity   Determining Biblical Answers to Worldview Questions

First, try to answer the questions above on your own by calling to mind your understood biblical answers. Then work with several others and discuss each question to determine biblical answers. Verify your answers using Scripture. This may take some time, but it is a worthwhile exercise that often leads to searching Scripture together. Afterward, sit down and write out a short paragraph of five to six sentences. This opening statement is a simple but meaningful expression of your philosophical bias. I consider it to be a preamble or introduction to the document. It will serve to remind you of your root or foundational beliefs that must inform each part of the document as you write about the aim of education, the nature of the student and learning, the role of the teacher in the learning event, and the nature and purpose of the curriculum. It is a good starting point.

My philosophy of education is informed by (or derived from) my philosophy of life (or worldview). I am a Christian, and as such I believe that . . .

people around us outside of Christ are helpless,
in need of salvation, in need of a reconciliation
with their creator. A human being is composed of
body, soul and spirit.

A person after death, their soul will leave
their body. either condemn to hell
or reserved a home in heaven

yes, our source of truth is God
inspired word our authority.
it gives us a knowledge and
understanding of God

- we have a sense of morality
since we were created in the
image of God
We know what is right and wrong.

• human history: is the affairs of man
and their thinking and enlightment,

.

Gen 1:27 = created man in his own image.
Gen 1:26
ps. 139:14 I am fearfully and wonderfully made:
Mathew 6:26: we have value
Gen 2:7 = formed out of dust
2 Timo 3:16
Colossian 1:23 Reconciled

3 | Defining Education

Training, Learning, and Education

In the past, educators have used several terms interchangeably without clarifying differences. Among these terms are *training, learning,* and *education.*

Activity | **Define or Describe Training, Learning, and Education**

The Bible does address some of these terms, and a study of the use of the words in Scripture from the Hebrew and Greek texts might be very productive. The term "education" is not used in Scripture, although the concept is widely addressed. We will use our common English understandings as we define education.

Take a minute or two and try to define or describe the three words (concepts) *training, learning,* and *education,* and then try to diagram the relationship among the three. When my students do this, I have several of them draw their diagrams on the chalk board, white board, or Smart Board. Then I ask other students in the class to interpret the diagrams. After "reading" and explaining the diagram, the person who drew it reads his definitions. The class determines whether or not the diagram depicts the definitions. While it is a fun activity, it does not take long to discover that not all students define or describe education the same way. This is an activity that the analytic philosopher might applaud. It reminds us to make sure, as much as possible, that we are communicating clearly with others by revealing our working definition or description of the concept under review.

How does Christian Ed fall with these terms

Try to define or describe *training, learning,* and *education:*

- *Training: passing down truths to someone, enabling, preparing them.*] *requires a mentor* | *day to day mundane skills.*

- *Learning: the studying of truths, facts, ideas*

- *education: study of different topics.*
  knowledge: information
  wisdom: knowledge applied

Defining Education | **19**

In the space below, try to diagram the relationship between *training, learning,* and *education:*

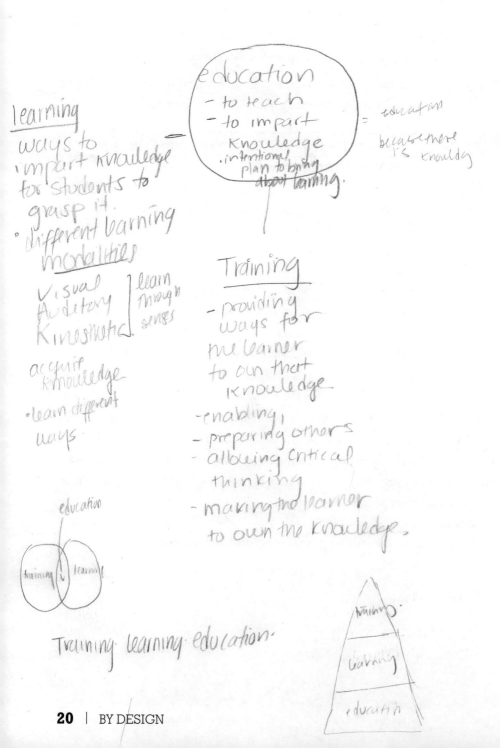

learning

ways to impart knowledge for students to grasp it.

· different learning modalities

Visual
Auditory   ] learn through senses
Kinesthetic

acquire knowledge

· learn different ways.

education
- to teach
- to impart knowledge
.intentional plan to bring about learning.

= education because there is knowledge

Training

- providing ways for the learner to own that knowledge

- enabling,
- preparing others
- allowing critical thinking
- making the learner to own the knowledge.

education

training ⋃ learning

Training learning education.

Training
learning
education

Defining the Terms

Here are some brief definitions that are acceptable in our discipline: *[handwritten: process meat information in mind]*

Learning is an interactive, continuous, organizing and reorganizing process *[handwritten: bring permanent change]* that leads to a relatively permanent change in thinking and acting. (This improves upon the behaviorist's definition that ignores mental processes and states that learning is simply a relatively permanent change in behavior.) *[handwritten: learning ↓ brings change]*

Education is a *deliberate* attempt to bring about learning. *[handwritten: purpose]*

Training is a deliberate attempt to bring about learning that leads to automatic responses to certain stimuli (skills / unreflective activities—a certain kind of learning). *[handwritten: especifically planning; stimuli = critical thinking; produces a change.]*

One thing is for sure: education is all about learning! Our concept of human learning is vital in a philosophy of education. Years ago, John Laska wrote a definition of education that has had staying power for as long as I have been teaching educational philosophy. In his book *Schooling and Education*, he defined education this way: "the deliberate attempt by the learner or by someone else to control…a learning situation in order to bring about the attainment of a desired learning outcome" (1976, p. 7).

Many have used Laska's definition, and worded it variously, but almost all who define education highlight the intentionality behind the process. Education is a planned and purposeful activity that leads to learning, transformation, or change. It is usually considered a process. Sometimes it is referred to as the product of this process ("I completed my high school education"). The relationship among the three terms might be diagrammed as follows:

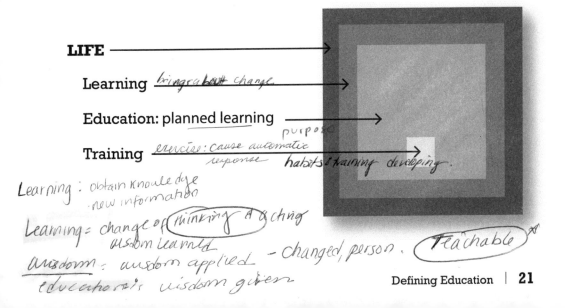

LIFE ⟶

Learning *[handwritten: brings about change.]* ⟶

Education: planned learning ⟶

Training *[handwritten: exercises: cause automatic response; purpose; habits & training developing.]*

[handwritten: Learning : obtain knowledge · new information]

[handwritten: Learning = change of (thinking & acting) wisdom learned — changed person. (Teachable)]

[handwritten: wisdom = wisdom applied educator's wisdom given]

Education is a subset of learning; therefore, the focus of an educational philosophy must be on learning. It is important to declare in your document how you describe learning. What kind of learning do you wish to promote—rote memory, concepts, understandings, actions, or what?

What Kind of Learning Do You Plan to Promote?

If you ask teachers this question, you will get responses in keeping with their educational perspective. Some will champion the subject matter, basic skills, tools for learning, or basics in mathematics and the language arts. Others will discuss how they wish to have students determine what they want to learn and then create projects and problem-solving activities that fit. You can quickly discern which of these ideas might be labeled "traditional" and which might be labeled "progressive" if you were chatting in the teacher's lounge. One of our tasks as we develop our educational philosophy is to determine what matters most: content or experiences, knowledge or action, cultural and general literacy or student interests. In solving this problem, we can get help from our underlying Christian roots informed by Scripture.

Activity | Research

What kind of learning seems to be promoted in the Bible? Can that view be generalized to all human learning in the various subject areas of the school curriculum? Using precepts and examples in the Scriptures, solve the problem and answer the questions above. Use the passages listed below, or any Scripture or line of reasoning you wish.

Precepts: Propositional statements or truth claims about education spoken/written directly

Examples: Teaching of Christ, the apostle Paul, or God the Father (with Israel, for example)

Some Scriptures to use: *knowledge – understanding → change → changes – love/fruit.*

Colossians 1:9, 10 (quoted below) *"filled with knowledge of will, wisdom, spiritual increasing of knowledge. understanding*

Deuteronomy 6:1–8 *→ words in me – teach them – become part of this person. hear – do it. keep in heart*

Joshua 1:8 *= meditate day and night / way to observe and do them.*

Philippians 4:8, 9 – *learned, received, heard, seen, DO*

Hebrews 5:14 *= appropriate level understood, to discern*

Colossians 1:9, 10 is a prayer of the apostle Paul for the people of Colossae, asking that they might learn the word of God a certain way. Use this passage and any others above that you wish to explore.

Education: purposely plan to bring about Learning

Learning: comes about if the student is CHANGED — will affect heart and actions.

learn - knowledge   *understanding = ends in the heart.*
                           principles/situations.

For this reason, since the day we heard about you, we have not stopped praying for you and asking God to fill you with the knowledge of his will through all spiritual wisdom and understanding. And we pray this in order that you may live a life worthy of the Lord and may please him in every way: bearing fruit in every good work, growing in the knowledge of God. — Colossians 1:9,10

Drawing on your brief study of Scripture, answer the following question:

Is learning a matter of remembered content/information, a matter of process/action, or something else? What do you think?

Now write: Education (planned, purposed learning) is portrayed in Scripture as…

learn & study   Education is portrayed as the imparting of
put to action   knowledge and understanding that brings
     a change in the life of the individual.
     This education is able to produce fruit,
       is able expand, to produce an impact.
       There is always a growing learning
       process than never ceases.
   education = Brings about a change.
       Knowing and understanding brings
          change in the individual

Let's look again at the prayer of the apostle Paul.

For this reason, since the day we heard about you we have not stopped praying for

you, and asking God to fill you with the *knowledge* of his will, through all spiritual
                              Know

wisdom and *understanding*.
     Understand

And we pray this in order that you may *live a life worthy of the Lord* and please him
                      Do (action)

in every way: *bearing fruit in every good work and growing in the knowledge of God.*
                Result: change

The apostle prayed that learning would bring about change in thinking *and* acting.

Several years ago, the state in which I work sent out a memorandum, requiring universities that had schools of education to make sure that their students included the state standards on all lesson plans and to make sure that prospective teachers wrote lesson objectives in terms of what the student will **know**, **understand**, and

Knowledge - mind   *process happens that*
Understanding - heart.   *leads to understanding.*

be able to **do**. (They did not cite the Scripture above but came up with a similar conclusion about learning.) Objectives should lead to fruitful learning that leads to a relatively permanent change in knowledge, understanding, and action on the part of the student. Interesting!

In writing your document and including the kind of learning you will intentionally promote, you might express your thinking something like this:

- Education is planned and purposed learning. *(MuST have an produce/ to have an impact objective)*
- Learning is a relatively permanent or enduring change in thinking and acting.

- Change occurs when the student takes in new information, processes and understands it, and can retrieve and use it. This kind of learning leads to enduring change!

Which pop label, *traditional* or *progressive*, is more nearly right as judged by your view informed by a biblical perspective? Is it the traditionalists, who focus on knowing and content, or is it the progressivists, who focus on process and action? Did you conclude that neither traditional nor progressive views seem to espouse a complete description of learning when you compare their views to one informed by biblical writers, such as Paul? The kind of learning Paul wished to promote leads to information, knowledge, and skills that are processed, understood, and stored in memory, for retrieval and use in life. This is one good reason—there will be others—to resist using the labels *traditional* or *progressive* to describe a philosophy of education informed by a biblical worldview.

4 | Determining the Aim or *End* of Education

If education is intentional, on purpose, planned learning, the question follows: For what purpose do we educate? How do we go about determining the "aim of education"? In *The Philosophical Bases of Education*, Robert Rusk writes that the "aim of education is relative to the aim of life."

As you read some of the quotes below written by educators describing the aim or overarching target for education, note how they have come to an understanding concerning the aim of education. From their perspective, why do we have schools? Why spend billions of dollars to education the children and youth of America (or any country, for that matter)? For what purpose do we teach reading, writing, arithmetic, and whatever? For what ultimate purpose do we educate? See if you can detect the underlying philosophy of life that informs these educational aims.

The Aim of Education: A Historical Perspective

A few years ago, I read the following letter in a local newspaper in September, right before the opening of school. It is written to teachers on the first day of school from a retiring principal who had survived the Holocaust. It was included in the epilogue of the book *Teacher and Child* by Haim Ginott as well. Read the letter below and critique the principal's aim of education. What is he offering his teachers as the overriding aim of education?

> Dear Teachers, I am a survivor of a concentration camp. My eyes saw what no person should witness: Gas chambers built by learned engineers, children poisoned by educated physicians, infants killed by trained nurses, women and babies shot and burned by high school and college graduates. So, I am suspicious of education. My request is: Help your students to become more human. Your efforts must never produce learned monsters, skilled psychopaths, educated Eichmanns. Reading, writing and arithmetic are important only if they serve to make our children more human (1972, p. 317).

What do you think this retiring principal is trying to say? Does his general concern resonate with you? Would you word your aim the same way? Ask yourself how you might modify or add to the aim if you were giving a speech or writing a letter to teachers. Why might you modify or add to his aim? This will help you begin to think about the aim of education from your own perspective.

Twentieth-century philosopher and educator Robert Maynard Hutchins (a Perennialist in educational philosophy) expressed his thoughts about aims of education in his book *Education for Freedom*. What is the aim of education according to Hutchins?

> Now wisdom and goodness are the aim of higher education. How can it be otherwise? Wisdom and goodness are the end of human life. . . How can we talk about preparing men for life unless we ask what the end of life may be? At the base of education, as at the base of every human activity, lies metaphysics (1943, pp. 23–24).

Notice that Hutchins connects the aim of education to the aim of life, just as Rusk did when writing about the philosophical bases of education. Writers often use the term the "end" of life to refer to the aim of life (rather than to death).

In the seventeenth century, John Milton (1608–1674) wrote his thoughts about the aim of education in the *Tractate on Education*, first published in 1644, now in the Harvard Classics:

> The end then of learning is to repair the ruins of our first parents by regaining to know God aright, and out of that knowledge to love Him, to imitate him, to be like Him, as we may the nearest, by possessing our souls of true virtue, which being united to the heavenly grace of faith, makes up the highest perfection (1909–14).

What is Milton's aim of life and aim of education?

[handwritten: Father of Modern Ed.]

In the 1600s, John Amos Comenius, considered to be the Father of Modern Education, wrote about educational aims in the book, *School of Infancy*:

> The useful purpose of all knowledge is to manifest the glory of God and to inspire man to love all that is good. In short the purpose for which youth ought to be educated is threefold: Faith and Reverence, Uprightness in Morals, and Knowledge of Language and Arts. These *[handwritten: Faith in God]* *[handwritten: character]* are to be taken in the precise order they appear and not inversely (1896, pp.10–11).

What is the aim of education from Comenius' viewpoint?

Where might the aim below have been posted for students and teachers to read and pursue?

[handwritten notes:]
(1) Faith & Reverence
   • Christianwalk.

(2) Uprightness in moral
   behavior
   character
   control
   way to act
   right from wrong

(3) Knowledge of language
   arts
   Academic

Let every student be plainly instructed and earnestly pressed to consider well the main end of his life and studies is to know God and Jesus Christ which is eternal life, John 17:3, and therefore to lay Christ in the bottom, as the only foundation of all sound knowledge and learning (Rules of Harvard College, 1642).

Notice that in each of the stated or implied aims of education above, the aim of life is addressed as well. As you address the aim of education for your philosophy of education document, you will ask, "What is the aim of life according to a Christian worldview, and how will that aim inform the aim of education?"

Plato, perhaps writing the thoughts of Socrates, lays out an overall aim for education when he writes: "If you ask what is good in general of education (*paideia*), the answer is easy: Education produces good men, and good men act nobly." His aim of education could be worded as the engendering or producing of the good and noble citizen. How do the aims of Milton, Comenius, and seventeenth-century Harvard compare or contrast with those of Plato? Why do you suppose that is true?

Activity | Discussion

If you are working with a partner or colleague, discuss the questions in the above paragraph. Locate other aims suggested in education text books or on the Internet, and evaluate these as well.

Current Aims of Education in Twenty-First-Century America and Other Countries of the World

Often referred to in schools of education when discussing the aim of education is Neil Postman's treatise on educational aims, *The End of Education*. In his book, he lays out the importance of having some organizing overall aim in order to provide meaning to education: "The truth is that schools cannot exist without some reason for its being, and in fact there are several gods our students are presently asked to serve" (1996, p. 27). Postman describes a "god" as a common narrative that all buy into as a part of the common good, "a comprehensive narrative about what the world is like, how things got to be the way they are, and what lies ahead" (p. 6). But he goes on to say that the current narratives that seem to inform the prevailing aim of education "do not serve us well and may lead to the end of public schooling" (p. 61). In fact, "both students and teachers lack a narrative to provide profound meaning to their lessons" (p. 51).

While Postman's conclusion might be true and the unavoidable outcome of a pluralistic society for public schools, it should not be true for private Christian schools. Christian schools should have a *narrative* that will "provide profound meaning to their lessons." The Christian narrative (worldview) serves as a powerful integrating force to provide meaning to all human endeavors, including learning, as it focuses on the ultimate purpose of human life and connects that purpose to the ultimate purpose of education. Do you agree?

Postman decries the narratives of education aimed at preparing for jobs alone. He warns educators not to promote the current mantra that "if you pay attention in school, and do your homework, and score well on tests, and behave yourself, you will be rewarded with a well-paying job when you are done" (p. 27). That aim, in summary, is competent entry into the economic life of the community. Jobs, consumerism, and technology seem to Postman to be the narratives of the day, and he believes that these have led to the "crisis in education." Why are jobs, consumerism, and technology the current aims in education? The answer is because they are part of the current narrative of life, the aim of life espoused by so many, at least in America—a good job leads to money, and money leads to having things, and things bring happiness, and happiness is the "end" of the good life.

So we ask, "How do I as an individual begin to express the aim of education? Am I writing for a school? Am I writing for the entire educational enterprise in my country, or what?" Well, the good news is that when writing a personal philosophy of education, you are writing your personal beliefs that will impact your life's work as an educator. The written aim is to keep you on target as to what is important in the planned curriculum and learning events of the school. It will help you answer the question, "Why this rather than that?" To stimulate your thinking, here is a typical aim written and found in various forms in foundations of education textbooks. This aim was first written in the early 1900s, renewed in the 1930s, and is still operative today as an American educational aim. See if you can determine the aim stated in the following quote and try to write it in your own words:

Education in a democracy should develop in each individual the knowledge, interests, ideals, habits and powers whereby he will find his place and use that place to shape both himself and society toward ever nobler ends.

Please write in your own words the aim expressed in the quote above.

> This man is being educated for the good himself but most importantly the profit of society. Society ultimately wins when a person is educated. The individual becomes well-rounded individual shaped by the education and is able to shape his society for a good cause

When I ask my students to write the (aim) found in this paragraph, they write something like this: "Education is for the personal development of the individual so that he or she can contribute to the society." Please evaluate their response.

> Education is able to produce fruit in the life of a person. He is able to use the skills, principles knowledge and wisdom to bring glory to God and apply it in the community.

To be sure, both personal development and contribution to society are goals in American education; however, the end of education or overarching aim expressed above is not the person in society, the person as an individual, or the society alone. It is, rather, some "nobler ends." Why, in a pluralistic society, would the writers of this quote not specify these "nobler" ends? Why do so "few" (according to Rusk cited earlier) formulate an aim of education, even though serious educators agree there must be one?

The answer is connected to how one goes about determining the aim. First, one must determine what is the aim or chief end of life, or (as Aristotle put it) the *summum bonum* of life—the supreme good from which all else is derived. In a pluralistic society where many different worldviews are represented in the public arena and many different aims of life are espoused, this becomes a problem. But not so for a Christian teacher or for Christian schools or other private schools, where all stakeholders should be able to agree on a common narrative of life or worldview. In fact, one of the main reasons for beginning this writing journey with a preamble that addresses your basic Christian beliefs is to provide a foundation for your entire document, including a foundation for the aim of education.

Try to determine, either by yourself or with some others, what a Christian view of the **aim of life** might be. For what purpose are we created and placed on this planet? Who are we as humans, and why are we here? You may need to come back and tweak this part of the philosophy after you examine and systematize your thoughts about the nature of the student and learning. After you have determined the aim of life, try to relate that aim to the aim of education. Remember that education is purposed and planned learning.

Write your thoughts here:

> Aim of education to equip, establish, build
> future leaders to stand in their communities
> for what is right. Education should have equipped them to
> fulfill their future tasks. The education should train them.
> They should be able to excel in life due to the byproduct of
> their education.

In *Education for Human Flourishing*, Paul Spears and Steven Loomis (2009) address, among other issues, the aim of education. Here is a sampling of what they might say to Neil Postman, who decried the economic focus of education. Postman might agree in part.

> While education does have utility, many educators believe that any utility derivable from education is secondary to higher and nobler ends. We live for truth, goodness, beauty and the achievement of proper conceptions of freedom. We also live for deeper relationships with others and a sustainable one with the created universe. We also live to know and understand God. Yes, choosing a vocation and getting a job are important byproducts of education. Yet the aim of a liberal education is "to develop the mind and character in making choices between truth and error, between right and wrong" (p. 173).

Notice that Spears and Loomis describe the "nobler" ends. They do not just drop into the conversation some nebulous, nondescript "nobler end" without describing the content of that end. Read their comment again and describe the nobler ends from their viewpoint.

- Character comes first
- One's moral development
- educated society

- truth
- goodness
- relationships

You may wish to pause and do some study on your own at this point. Then finish this sentence:

I believe the aim of life is … glorify God | serve God.

love God. be ambassadors.

and therefore the aim of education should be: points students to the one of all knowledge

An aim of education unpacked in part from this quote in *Education for Human Flourishing* might be something like this:

> **The aim of education is to promote human flourishing, the living out of what God intended His created image bearers to be:** by pursuing truth about God, His universe, and humankind (ourselves and others); by knowing, understanding, and effectively using knowledge and skills for wise living; and by acting ethically; thereby growing personally and serving and benefiting society—all to the glory of God, the ultimate aim and first principal or *summum bonum* of LIFE!

Aim of Education: Human Flourishing

What do I mean by "flourishing"? *Eudaimonia* (you-die-monia) is a Greek word commonly translated as *happiness*. Aristotle used this as his *summum bonum* of life. In our popular usage, happiness refers to a joyful or pleasurable state of mind. However, *eudaimonia* rarely has this meaning. It is often translated as *human flourishing*. Human flourishing means different things to different worldviews. For the Christian, it seems to mean developing fully as God intended His creatures to develop: as a flourishing green tree, blessed.

> But blessed is the man who trusts in the Lord, whose confidence is in Him. He will be like a tree planted by the water that sends out its roots by the stream. It does not fear when heat comes; its leaves are always green. It has no worries in the year of drought and never fails to bear fruit. —Jeremiah 17:7–8

Here is a new meaning of "going green!" One translation of the Hebrew word for *green* is *flourishing*.

Sink down knowledge to heart ♥

- head: knowledge
- heart: sinking becomes knowledge. ⇒
    - brings understanding / what value, what prioritize, what they respond
    - producing action / change

Aim of Education: Head or Heart?

Here is another question to consider when writing the aim: Do you think that the aim of education is a matter of the heart or the head? Educational writers and philosophers differ on their emphasis, head or heart.*

What might the Tin Woodman and the Scarecrow say about the head versus the heart in L. Frank Baum's *The Wonderful Wizard of Oz*?

> "Why didn't you walk around the hole?" asked the Tin Woodman.
>
> "I didn't know enough," replied the Scarecrow, cheerfully. "My head is stuffed with straw, you know, and that is why I am going to Oz to ask him for some brains."
>
> "Oh, I see," said the Tin Woodman. "But, after all, brains are not the best things in the world."
>
> "Have you any?" inquired the Scarecrow.
>
> "No, my head is quite empty," answered the Woodman. "But once I had brains, and a heart also; so having tried them both, I should much rather have a heart…"
>
> "All the same," said the Scarecrow, "I shall ask for brains instead of a heart; for a fool would not know what to do with a heart if he had one."
>
> "I shall take the heart," returned the Tin Woodman; "for brains do not make one happy, and happiness is the best thing in the world."
>
> —L. Frank Baum, *The Wonderful Wizard of Oz*

While neither of the characters in the *The Wonderful Wizard of Oz* has a very good philosophy of life, they do raise a very good question for those who often pit strong academics against personal development or spiritual development. But is this a false dichotomy? The twentieth century saw a pendulum swing between two poles: personal development as the aim of education on one side and academics as the aim on the other. At various periods of time, one or the other won out. Usually the prevailing educational philosophy of the culture determines the answer.

*Note: James Sire, in *Naming the Elephant* (2004), and J. P. Moreland, in *Love Your God with All Your Mind* (1997), take two slightly different points of view on the "head vs. heart" issue, and it would serve the reader well to research these two views.

Traditionalists often focus on academics (cultural literacy, content, core knowledge, scholarship). Progressivists often focus on personal and social development (self-esteem, problem-solving, and decision-making for life issues). In the late 1990s, the Association of Supervision and Curriculum Development presented its yearbook on this very topic. Notice the title: *Rethinking Educational Change with the Heart and Mind* (ed. Hargreaves 1997). The title is telling. It clearly points to a "rethinking" of this important issue in education. Now it is your turn to rethink!

| **Activity** | **Head and Heart in the Twenty-First Century** |

Which side has been winning in the twenty-first century? For example, what has been the focus of the No Child Left Behind legislation, the Standards movement, or the Common Core Curriculum movement?

What would you like to say about the place of the heart and the head in your aim of education? Be ready to add your thoughts to what you have already written. You may want to jot some notes here.

> *The 'mind' will receive knowledge which will impact the heart and bring change produce fruit as it impacted the individual.*

If the aim of education is to promote the full development of each human being as he/she was intended to be (an image bearer of the God of the universe), we must help each individual student develop in all areas: cognitively, socially, emotionally, physically, and spiritually. Head and heart are both vital considerations in education informed by a Christian worldview: "Love the Lord your God with all your **heart** and with all your **soul** and with all your **mind**. *This* is the first and greatest commandment" (Matthew 22:37–38, emphasis mine). *This*: singular.

You are now ready to add your developed aim of education to your opening preamble and to the definitions and descriptions of philosophy and education. If our aim is to glorify God by promoting growth and development in His creatures, we must understand human beings and learning. We must understand our role in the process, and we must understand how we plan the curriculum to reach the aim. These issues form the heart of the philosophy of education document and are addressed in Section Two. *Both important.*   *head: academics*
heart: seeds grow.

Both mind & heart

Educational Responsibility

There is a sociological issue that is often included in a philosophy of education as a question. The question can be addressed under the aim, under the role of the teacher, or wherever the writer thinks it fits best. Here is the question: ***Who has primary responsibility for the education of the child?***

Who do you think has primary responsibility for the education of the child—not necessarily for all of the teaching of the child, but the responsibility first and foremost for seeing that the aim of education is fulfilled?

What Do You Think?

Where might you find a statement in a government document like the one below? What country, state, or locale?

"The natural rights of parents to custody and control of their children are subordinate to the power of the state to provide for the education of their children. Laws providing state education of the children are for the protection of the state itself."

When I show my class this quote and ask the question above, they often answer that it might be one of the states in the U.S.A., the federal government, or perhaps Cuba, the former Soviet Union, or China. Why might they say that?

Actually, the quote above was part of the Ohio revised school code, p. 195 Section 7106 of Compulsory Education Law. (It is no longer in the code.)

It was thought at the time the original code was written that the welfare of the minor child was so important that the state had the right to interfere with the freedom of the parents. Loyalty to America was at stake. This was during a time when the "melting pot" concept of America was very popular. Compulsory education was essential in the process.

What do most of the states in the USA hold related to this issue? Research the issue on the Internet. See if you can find what your state holds in relation to this question.

What about the United Nations in its declaration of the "Rights of the Child"? Do you think the UN considers the government, the family, or the national or local church as having primary responsibility for the education of the child? Select one and write it here.

> The job to train and provide the right education for the children should be based on the parents.

Now read from that document in the box and see if you were correct.

> "He [the child] shall be given an education which will promote his general culture and enable him, on a basis of equal opportunity, to develop his abilities, his individual judgement, and his sense of moral and social responsibility, and to become a useful member of society. The best interests of the child shall be the guiding principle of those responsible for his education and guidance; that responsibility lies in the first place with his parents."
>
> —*Declaration of the Rights of the Child UN General Assembly, 1959 (principle 7)*

Activity **Agree or Disagree**

1. All public schools are government-controlled (by states in the USA).

   Yes, they control what is taught and propagated in the school.

2. Some Christian schools, other private schools, and home schools are parent-controlled.

   Yes, They should be the parents should know what their children are being taught.

3. Some Christian, parochial, and other religious schools are church-controlled.

   The church can control but the parents should always know exactly what their children are being taught.

The Issue

What God-ordained institution has primary responsibility for the education of the child? This is not only a contextual modifier, but a sociological issue that has implications for educating the youth of any country. How do we determine who has primary responsibility for the education of children in a pluralistic society (or in any society), and how might this impact what we do as educators?

Activity | A Biblical View of Primary Responsibility

Decide on the answer to the question as you now view it, and then examine your answer in light of a biblical view of the institutions listed below, all of which are God-ordained and all of which have taken, at one time or another, the responsibility for the education of the child.

Who has primary responsibility for the education of children? (not necessarily the responsibility to *teach* them, but ultimate responsibility for seeing that the aim of education is carried out)

☑ Parents/family

☐ Church

☐ State

First, determine the function for each of these institutions, all of which are found in Scripture. Then, try to connect each institution and its function to schooling.

What is the God-ordained function of the family?

• The parents are to teach, nurture and model to their children a heart for the things of God.

What is the God-ordained function of the church?

To be a pillar of truth. light in darkness. A spiritual hospital beacon of light & truth, follow-great commission.

What is the God-ordained function of the government? *(keep order)*

Keep law and order. punish righteous unpunish righteous.

Here are some clues, but a brief study of these biblically valid institutions will help you discover the functions of each. Among other things, the following may be considered.

each have responsibility

The family—Responsibility for individual character of the child (Deuteronomy 6) *Teaching training nurturing. (choosing schools to partner up.)*

The church—Responsibility for the corporate character of the body of Christ (Ephesians 4)

The government—Responsibility for the corporate character of society (Romans 13)

There is a place for all three institutions in the task of human flourishing. However, one must have "primary" responsibility. What do you think? Write your choice and conclusions here.

- Primary responsability would be to live to love and please God, to serve Him, point students to the Lord.

Write what you, as a teacher, will or will not do if indeed you believe what you have written above. Think for a minute about how your belief will impact a teacher-parent conference. How might your belief affect a pastor whose church has a Christian school but not all of the congregation utilizes the school? Many in that church put their kids in public schools or home school, for example. How does your view compare to the bishop of Baltimore, who in the late 1800s declared that every church should have a parish school and congregants should send their children to these schools, at least until the age of 12? How would your view hold up in conversation with a person who said that the academic life of the child is a key to a strong society and is therefore accomplished best by the government, the primary stakeholder in creating a good society?

- To teach the children about God, His word, His plan, His will for their lives.

It may surprise you that in the recent past some professional educators advocated an adversarial relationship between the teacher and the family. "Get them off your back! You are the professional," was the main idea of an article I was required to read during my doctoral program.

What are you thinking about this issue? Some of my students think like this before they do some examination of the issue: "Well, the family is not doing its job today and many kids do not go to church, so I believe the primary responsibility for educating the child lies with the government or state-controlled schools."

While much of that statement is probably true, and the sentiment is understood, should that change the underlying answer to the question of responsibility? Why or why not?

- No, because we are accountable to God.

Teacher sees their role as being entrusted with children partnering with parents. working together

Because I believe that the primary responsibility for the education of the child lies with

(select one of the three options: parent, church, state) _____ *parent* ,

I will _____ ~~parent~~ *assistined* or will not ~~use state~~ _____

or the school should or should not _____ ~~always~~ *turn students from parents*

Note: This is not an opportunity to scold one institution or another for not fulfilling its God-ordained function. It is a time to state what you believe and how that belief will inform **your** behavior as a teacher or administrator.

Section One Conclusion

It might be worthwhile to stop here and take some time to write the entire first sections of your document. Use the outline bullets below to help frame your thoughts.

- **Preamble:** The preamble serves as your stated foundation, roots, or bias. It is a brief summary of your underlying Christian worldview.

- **Define/describe the terms Philosophy and Education:**

  - Describe or define the concept of a **general philosophy of life** or worldview.

  - The decision to use either a full-blown root philosophy or a Christian worldview that answers the big questions of life is yours. Use what fits your background best.

  - Define education for your audience or reader. Remember to think about **education** as planned and purposeful learning.

  - Ask yourself what **kind of learning** you intend to promote (content, process, or what?).

  - **The aim of education** and its relationship to the aim of life from a Christian perspective.

  - The sociological question: Who has **primary responsibility** for the education of the child?

Section Two Introduction

"The great glory and strength of pluralism is that it compels the holder of any belief to measure its truthfulness against alternative interpretations. The great hazard of pluralism is the faulty deduction, in the name of tolerance, that all beliefs can be equally true. It is ultimately truth, not popularity or rights, that determines destiny."

—Ravi Zacharias, *Deliver Us From Evil*, p. 82

The Key Elements of an Educational Philosophy

The Nature of the *Student* and Learning

The Role of the *Teacher* in Promoting Learning

The Nature and Purpose of the *Curriculum* and Learning

What is the nature of the human being and learning? What is the nature of knowledge and knowing? How are these educational understandings brought together in a classroom in order to promote effective learning? How does the curriculum promote human flourishing that glorifies the Creator? Section Two will assist teachers and prospective teachers in examining, clarifying, analyzing, developing, and systematizing their beliefs about the student and learning, the teacher, and the curriculum, so that the end product will be a document or manifesto that declares the instructional philosophy that informs their behaviors as teachers. To begin the overview of the key elements of school education—the student, the teacher, and the curriculum—let's take a look at some typical educational mantras or sayings from popular educational journals and practicing teachers.

Educational Mantras

What are some of the typical beliefs about students and school success that reign supreme in houses of education today? Some come directly from the culture in general, while others are promoted in college and university schools of education and professional development workshops.

Part of the examination of your current beliefs is to reflect upon content and experiences you have internalized from previous courses and professional development workshops, and then to intentionally submit your beliefs to biblical scrutiny. Truth, not popularity, is the goal.

Activity | Pause, Think, and Write

To see how educators are influenced by the culture in which we work or study, read and evaluate these teacher "mantras."

[handwritten left margin: humanist]

- "You can be anything you want to be if you want it badly enough!" *[handwritten: ✱ "Motivational"]*
- "Just believe in yourself, and all will be well."
- "You must turn inward before turning outward; love yourself before you love others."
- "Together now: let's say, 'I am somebody!' 'I am somebody!'"

You might be able to think of others you have heard over and over again in the field of education. If so, write them here.

[handwritten:]
1- God made me differently. Doesn't mean that's God wants for you.
2- humanism = removing God and placing self
3-

[handwritten:] "Follow your heart" not to do best = lazy   Do better.

[handwritten:] Teacher: help student Think biblically

[handwritten:] "aim at something"

These educational "mantras" are stated over and over again in schools around the world on a daily basis. What do you think they mean, and how do they stand up to a biblically informed worldview? Evaluate these statements in terms of reason, logic, human biology, and a biblical view of the "human being." Do you agree or disagree with them. Defend your decision.

[handwritten:] These mantras are anti-God. They take God out of the focus in children's lives.

[handwritten:] he alone gives me strength

Let's look at some of these statements together. First: **"You can be anything you want to be if you want it badly enough."**

I heard this statement just a few years back at a girl's Christian high school basketball championship. The game was neck and neck with first one team up and then the other. Exciting! But then, of course, one team won, and just by two points. (It is a game with winners and losers!) The two teams responded, one with the thrill of victory and the other with the agony of defeat.

The coach of the losing team called his players over and shouted at them, *"You didn't want it bad enough!"* Now, I knew that was not true. They wanted to win that game more than anything else on that day. Just as shocking as the coach equating desire with victory was what he did after his scold. He sent the girls to the locker room without shaking hands with the winning team, whose members were waiting on the sideline. What message is he sending to these girls? Did it reflect a biblical view of winning or losing? Did it even portray common courtesy? What character lesson is at hand? Have you ever told a student that if he tries very hard, he will win? While it is certainly biblical to declare that we are to do everything heartily as unto the Lord, that does not ensure that the results always will be victory. We work hard to honor the Lord (a biblical view of things) and leave the results to Him. I wonder what the view of a human as having "unlimited or infinite potential" does to a person's human personality when he finds that it is not true. But this mantra is a constant in many schools today.

Students absorb their worldview answers through various means in a school classroom: the words and attitudes of the teacher and other students, the curriculum, and the general culture of the school. I have a child's coloring book that is all about self-esteem. On the cover are three children: a baseball player, a scholar, and a musician. All three have a button pinned to their shirts that reads, "#1." Think about that. Can every student be #1? Even the cat in the picture is #1. What is the message? The creators of the book wrote a note to parents that included this sentiment. "We hope that [the coloring book] will be a positive influence on your child's early development." I concluded that it *will* be an influence—but perhaps not a positive one, especially if the child is never #1 in anything! How do we as Christian teachers encourage our students to do their best and be all that God wants them to be without telling them that unless they are the first chair in the orchestra, the top baseball player on the team, or the student with the highest grade point average, they have little worth? How sad. Beliefs about human beings and their human characteristics matter!

The second common mantra is: **"Just believe in yourself!"**

This is a corollary statement to statement number one. I happened to see this statement in print in a teacher's lounge, written under the question to teachers: "Having difficulty with discipline in your classroom? Just believe in yourself." I have news for teachers. Believing in yourself is not sufficient for success in classroom discipline. You must know some strategies, the purpose of discipline, your students, and more.

Are you getting the point? We absorb the mantras of the educational culture without evaluating their fit with a biblical worldview. From a Christian perspective, we should have a healthy view of ourselves because we know that our worth and potential are grounded in the creatorship of God. As His creatures, created in His image, we are special, we are loved by Him. He wants us to flourish as humans, and He can use both our strengths and our weaknesses for His glory. When Moses was asked by God to lead the Israelites, he retorted with the question, "Who am I, that I should go to Pharaoh and bring the Israelites out of Egypt?" (Exodus 3:11) and the statement, "O Lord, I have never been eloquent . . . I am slow of speech and tongue" (Exodus 4:10). The Lord did not say to him, "Moses, just believe in yourself." His message to Moses was, "I will go with you. Who made your mouth?"

We are bombarded through media with the idea of "being anything we want to be" and "believing in ourselves." We need to examine these beliefs in light of who we are as human beings. To whom do we listen for our *own* instruction? Take for example the words of popular writer, speaker, and East/West thinker Deepak Chopra. He answers worldview questions including the question, "What is a human being?"

In his audiobook *Escaping the Prison of the Mind: A Journey From Here to Here*, Chopra said, "I know myself as the immeasurable potential of all that was, is, and will be. I am omnipresent, omniscient; I am eternal spirit that animates everything in existence" (1992, xxxi).

Chopra's conclusion: Unlimited human potential. I can be anything. Why? I am god.

Consider the prayers quoted by feminist Gloria Steinem a few years back. In the book *Revolution From Within: A Book of Self-Esteem* (1992), she appreciatively quotes the following prayers:

i found god in myself

& i loved her

i loved her fiercely

    —Ntozake Shange

The Lord of all

The knower of all

The beginning and end of all

The Self dwells in every heart.

    —Upanishads

After reading Steinem's book, a blogger shared:

"My favorite quote, so far, is Gloria Steinem citing Alan Watts . . . 'How is it possible...that a being with such sensitive jewels as the eyes, such enchanted musical instruments as the ears, and such fabulous arabesque of the nerves as the brain can experience itself as anything less than god?'"(Hoang 2012)

Or consider the self-proclaimed New Ager, Shirley MacLaine, who at the end of the twentieth century, concluded her book *Dancing in the Light* this way: "I know the god source exists, therefore it is; I know that I am part of the god source, therefore, I am that I am" (1985).

It appears that some popular writers in our culture during the last several decades hold a view of the self that places self in the center of their universe as god. Our culture influences our thinking. Teachers often succumb to whatever the majority is saying and convert these worldview beliefs into messages for the classroom, often unexamined. This may be true of Christian teachers as well as non-Christian.

No wonder teachers and administrators and parents often tell kids to believe in themselves. The message permeates our culture. A few months ago I saw a cute but interesting sign in an airport. It pictured Shrek with the caption, "Ogre Achiever. Believe in Yourself!" This was a message from the Foundation for a Better Life. Really?

The French Existentialist Jean Paul Sartre said it best for those who hold this view when he wrote in *Existential Psychoanalysis*, "Man is the being whose project is to be God" (1953, p. 66).

I checked Google for lessons on self-esteem. The lesson in the first result closed with the line, "Remember you can have anything in this world if you just believe in yourself." What do you as a teacher think and say concerning the self? How will your beliefs affect the students you teach?

The third typical saying is: **"You must turn inward before you turn outward; love yourself before you love others."**

How does this fit with a biblical worldview? This was a very popular saying 15–20 years ago, and it has not changed in our culture. Alan Bloom, author of *The Closing of the American Mind*, called this "mantra" a myth held by many of his students in the late twentieth century. Not many years later, sociologists labeled the children of the 80s the "Me" generation (for good reason). James Emery White, writing from a Christian perspective, calls this third statement not a myth but a challenge faced by the person who desires to develop a "mind for God." He calls it the challenge of "Narcissistic Hedonism" or the "I, me, and mine" syndrome (*A Mind for God*, p. 31).

How would you critique the third statement in the list of mantras, "love yourself first"? Have you ever heard the following lyrics? You might even be able to sing them! Invariably, when I speak to teachers who are 10 years or more out of college, some just begin to sing this song when I project it on the screen. The song became somewhat popular again after the death of Whitney Houston.

Everybody's searching for a hero	Inside of me
People need someone to look up to	The greatest love of all
I never found anyone to fulfill my needs	Is easy to achieve
So I learned to depend on me	Learning to love yourself
I found the greatest love of all	It is the greatest love of all

—"The Greatest Love of All" (*Creed and Masser, sung by the late Whitney Houston*)

If a pop star sings a song with beautiful music that is catchy and warm, the lyrics can get lost in the singing—but not in the mind. The message is clear, and if repeated enough, it begins to stick.

How does this song fit with or contrast with the following?

"'Love the Lord your God with all your heart and with all your soul and with all your mind.' This is the first and greatest commandment. And the second is like it: 'Love your neighbor as yourself.' All the Law and the Prophets hang on these two commandments" (Matthew 22:37–40).

The greatest love of all is the love of God and the love for God.

"Love each other as I have loved you. Greater love has no one than this, that he lay down his life for his friends" (John 15:12,13).

You may have heard the preschool song below used in many kindergartens today (sung to the tune of "Frère Jacques").

I am special,
I am special,
Look at me,
You will see,
Someone very special,
Someone very special,
It is me
It is me

> "Sometimes a culture can so imperceptibly absorb and transmit ideas into the consciousness that it is hard for those within it to be objective about the propriety of its practices when measured against a counter-perspective."
>
> —Ravi Zacharias, *Deliver Us From Evil*, p. 19

While the sentiment of human specialness is true and biblically accurate, at no place in the song would children get the "truth": that they are special because they are created by God and in His image. In fact, the last two lines teach incorrect grammar as well, and it might be far better to rewrite the lines to say and sing, "God made me!" "God made me!" I am special and I am "somebody" because of God's creative work and His ongoing work in my life.

The truth is that we are impacted by our culture, and we bring these culturally popular slogans or beliefs into our teaching without examining them in light of a biblical worldview. In writing a philosophy of education, it is essential that we examine our own currently held beliefs to see if they are consistent with a Christian philosophy of life. We are doing that in this section of our philosophy of education. We are looking at the nature of the human being. We are examining our current thoughts and beliefs, whether impacted by the pop "traditional" or "progressive" labels or current cultural mantras; and we are clarifying, modifying, or changing them to bring them into correspondence with the truth of God's Word. Truth is the goal.

interactive

Birth-5
5-12
12-15
16+   introduce to
         econ, history,
            religion.

- learning styles
- disability mental
- goals & abition
- foundational level

5 | Nature of the Student and Learning

Beginning with this chapter, an approach will be introduced and then used to think through the remaining elements of a philosophy of education. First, we will chart the generally held beliefs of traditional and progressive views in order to activate our thinking on the issue under study. Then we will explore and examine the currently held views and beliefs of the individual writing the document. (That would be you! What do you believe about the nature of the student and learning?) These beliefs will then be submitted to a brief analysis to determine whether or not they make sense with an informed biblical worldview. The goal is not only to write the beliefs that you have intentionally accepted, but also to examine whether or not they are consistent and coalesce with a biblical worldview. The ultimate goal is to be able to flesh out these beliefs in a classroom and to avoid being automatically sucked into the thinking of the culture. Therefore, some implications will be addressed throughout. *"follow your heart" Be careful what you're putting in classroom?*

Activity | Read and Respond

You are interviewing for a job at International Christian School, and the interview committee chair asks the following question: *"How would you describe human nature, and thus the nature of the student, as it relates to education?"*

What would you say? What is a human being? How will your beliefs impact what you will or will not do in a teaching situation in a school? Write the first thing that comes to mind.

Start this way: *I believe that the human* (student) *by nature* (born with characteristic) *is...*

created in the image of God
- *Human being a sinner, heart desperately wicked.*
- *I will not let students "explore" and learn, and do whenever they please.*
- *I will point students to their Redeemer*

Ask yourself whether or not what you have written first is the most important descriptor with which to begin. *The goal is the children's heart to not follow their hearts but to rather point them to the Redeemer of their heart.*

Nature of the Student and Learning | 47

My philosophy of education students do this in groups and usually come up with several categories such as: "created in the image of God," "interactive by nature," "developmental by nature," "morally responsible," "flawed because of the Fall and resulting sin nature," "individually different because of individual genetic makeup, specific family environment, and cultural and ethnic background." This list is not complete. You may think of others.

| Activity | Examine Traditional and Progressive Views |

Now take a few minutes and try to decide what many diehard* traditionalists would say about human nature and learning and what many diehard progressives might say. Use the blank chart for your comparison. Possible answers may be found in the completed chart that follows. Compare these to your own view.

Human Nature and Learning	
Traditional	**Progressive**
• can be successful if teaching is handled with the help of God's Word • To point children to Truth. • To give them hope in God. • To develop their gifts and talents for the glory of God. • the mind but also to feed the heart.	• Student makes choices for themselves • Student controls the classroom • student everything revolves around him or her.

*"Diehard," here, refers to one who holds almost exclusively to one or the other set of the beliefs of traditionalists or progressives.

Some possible answers may be found below. These are just examples. Compare these to your own view.

Human Nature and Learning	
Traditional *Structure*	**Progressive**
• Rational: natural capacity to think, to know, and to acquire knowledge and seek truth; the most important aspect of learners is their intellect or the mind. • Sensory learners • Passive rather than active in the learning event; they take into the mind information from outside • Morally flawed or morally neutral, and in need of moral instruction and guidance • Subject to natural law and therefore not free in their choices; morally neutral (Behaviorism) • Part of a great universal machine that can be programmed in a manner similar to computers (Behaviorism; Determinism) • A microscopic self who is in the process of becoming more like absolute self (Idealism)	• Possess a natural desire to learn and discover things about the world around them • Active rather than passive in the learning event; learning emerges primarily from within the learner • Experiencing individuals who are capable of using their intelligence to resolve problematic situations and contribute to society (Pragmatism) • A choosing agent, a free agent, and a responsible agent (Existentialism) • Capacity to increase in self-awareness and find and be themselves or to create themselves • Morally good or neutral: if good, restraint is not good, and children should be able to unfold their goodness; if neutral, children need moral education, usually through modeling (Dewey)

(handwritten notes: "structure belief system" above top-right; "Children unfold goodness.")

How does your view compare to the chart? Do you find some descriptors under each category with which you agree? If so, you may wonder whether it is of value to label your philosophy as "traditional" or "progressive." Write your thoughts before you go on to the next activity. If you were asked again whether you are traditional or progressive, you might consider answering this way: "*If by traditional you mean _____, then I am; I agree with that; however, if by traditional you mean _____, then I am not traditional.*" Do the same with progressive beliefs. This avoids being locked into a label and also avoids misunderstanding as you answer the question. You simply tell what you believe, and why.

Please respond to the following; circle your answer:

I believe all students learn alike! Agre or Disagree

I believe all students learn differently! Agree or Disagree

A large majority of teachers, especially teachers-to-be, will agree with the second statement but not the first, and most would label the second as a progressive belief. There might be very good reasons for thinking like that, but it may be helpful to ask a few questions.

[handwritten: focusing on differences will excuse you]

1. If you have a self-contained classroom of 25 students, what must you do if you believe just the second statement? Why? *[handwritten: Implement progressive ideas to cater to students learning]*

2. If you have 105 middle school or high school students in five different classes, what would you need to do if you held just to the second statement? *[handwritten: You will need to implement different learning tools]*

3. What might you do in your planning and preparation if you held to the first statement only? *[handwritten: • stick with the same method of lecturing + expecting student to learn.]*

What might be a better approach to thinking about students, one that fits with common sense in practice and the nature of the learner? Might it be worthwhile to consider commonalities as well as difference for practical and perhaps philosophical reasons? How would an understanding of both commonalities and differences help you to promote learning, and why? This is a good discussion question if you are working through this book with others.

[handwritten: •commonalities - varities - [Brain] very helpful to know.]

I recommend that you use a broad template to begin your thinking about the nature of the student and learning, one that will begin to make sense to you as you review all the ways you have studied human beings in your educational programs, professional development, teacher training, or your prior experiences. The template begins with commonalities and then addresses differences. Why do you think that, when examining human nature, I have included both (1) what all humans have in common, and (2) how humans are different? Bigge and Shermis help to clarify the description of the nature of the human and learning by beginning with comments about commonalities. They write in *Learning Theories for Teachers* that the focus on human learning is first and foremost about how *all humans learn* by nature:

It is essential to make clear that we are using the word *people* in a generic sense. This applies collectively to all members of the human species, and thus to all students at all levels of education and ability.

Furthermore, as used here, *innate* and *basic* are synonymous adjectives; both mean *original* or *unlearned*. Consideration of the basic nature of people would be quite simple were there but one answer. But interestingly there are several distinctly different and mutually opposed answers to this question, each enjoying a good deal of support (2004, p. 15).

Template for Commonalities and Differences in Human Nature

Various worldviews answer the questions, "What is a human being, and how do we learn?" very differently. How do we as Christians answer these questions? This will be the focus of the next three chapters. Here is a template to help organize your thoughts.

I. Commonalities (things that are true of all humans because we are born into the human family, rather than into the family of plants, animals, angels, or God)

    1 A. Special category of living things (why special?) *chapt 6*

    2 B. Moral nature (good, bad, neutral) *chap 6.*

    3 C. Actional nature (passive, active, interactive—these are mutually opposed)* *chapt 7 & 8*

    4 D. General developmental nature *chp. 7*

* The actional nature is the most difficult to understand and will be examined in chapter seven.

II. Differences (human differences by birth or developed over time, individual, and cultural)

    1 A. Individual developmental variance from the norm (statistical curve) *ch 9*

    2 B. Individual preferences and capacities in learning—brain or *ch. 9* experience-related—for example, learning styles and multiple intelligences, and cognitive processing

    3 C. Cultural and social forces that affect individuals and groups of *ch. 9* individuals

    4 D. Various other abilities and disabilities *ch. 9.*

Alone, with a pair, or in a group, talk through the above template and then record all of your own beliefs related to commonalities and differences. Use the template above.

Write your thoughts here:

handwritten notes:

- The teacher should be the leader, the one with authority.
- The students submit to the teacher.
- ✓ teacher accommodates their teaching according to students learning abilities.
- Teacher changes their methods of teaching but not the core values
- Teacher model to students.

We will develop each category using biblical references where possible, so as to be informed by our biblical worldview. This will serve to avoid glib statements memorized in the past about students and learning that might not have been examined and may actually be in conflict with a biblical view. It will help us to avoid unexamined cultural mantras and provide evidence for an informed choice of beliefs that should be reflected in practice.

Simply make your statements of belief as in a manifesto rather than presenting your beliefs as a theology paper or a persuasion paper with end notes and resources. Even though students in my classes use Scripture to inform their worldview, when they write their document they are not required to quote Scripture in the body. In conversation, however, they (and you) should be able to defend why you hold the beliefs you do from a Christian perspective, even citing biblical references when appropriate. In class, on a regular basis, I require my students to verbalize their beliefs and defend them from a Christian perspective. This is a good exercise for all teachers. The template on page 51 serves to create some pegs upon which to hang your thoughts. The outline represents various ways you may have studied human beings in the past.

6 | Commonalities: Special Creation and Moral Nature

Blaise Pascal, a seventeenth-century mathematician, warned in his *Pensées*:

It is dangerous to show a man too clearly how much he resembles the beast, without at the same time showing him his greatness. It is also dangerous to allow him too clear vision of his greatness without his baseness. It is even more dangerous to leave him in ignorance of both (as cited in Jeeves 2011, p. 192).

Commonalities

What comes to your mind as being the most important characteristic of a human being, true of all in the family of humankind, to consider in education? Write your choice here:

- Man has a soul, he was created by God. God's plan is for salvation of mankind
- In such plan, God has an specific plan for each of their life that will bring glory to God
- Man are to be God's-image bearer

I. Commonalities

    A. Special Creation

What does it mean to be a human and not a plant, animal, angel, or God? How might the category of humankind be described? What does it mean to be "created in the image of God?" What does it mean to bear the image of God? Try to describe the characteristics of God's image that we possess.

Humans Created to bear the image of God.

Activity | Write: The Image of God

Describe the characteristics of humans that might fit the description as image-bearers of God. For foundational thought, use the following Scripture references that declare the truth that humans are indeed created in the image of God.

Genesis 1:26, 27

we are to demonstrate to world _we reflect something of God's nature and character of rest of creation). Eg) goodness, love, mercy, justice._

Genesis 9:6

are called to care for all God has made share and develop creation. to make the most of it for His glory

Psalm 8:4

God has a desire to have a relationship and relationship with him

Notice in Genesis 1 the clear statement that God Himself makes about His creation of humans in His image and likeness. The declaration of the image of God in man is made again in Genesis 9 after the Fall and the horrendous wickedness that led to the flood in the days of Noah. Humans were still described as image-bearers, and although given the right to kill animals for food in Genesis 9, they are forbidden to kill humans. The reason given: "for in the image of God has God made man." The psalmist asks, "What is a human that God is mindful of him?" and then answers his own question: He is made a little lower than the heavenly beings, crowned with glory and honor, and made to rule over the works of God's hand (Psalm 8:4).

Activity | Write: Characteristics of the Image of God

Finish this sentence: _Among other things, wonderful and mysterious, a human being created in the image of God, possesses the following characteristics:_

1. _rational_
2. _emotion_
3. _soul_
4. _conscious_
5. _God's moral attributes_

Check your descriptors with those you will find below—some of which are typically found in textbooks or theology and Bible commentaries written on the topic of anthropology.

1. Responsible and accountable choosers—moral responsibility
2. Vice-regents—stewardship (care for God's creation)
3. Rational—thought, internal processing
4. Communicators—external verbalization of thoughts
5. Relational—social
6. Emotional—feelings
7. Creative
8. Possess consciousness and self-consciousness

Whatever else it means to be created in the image of God, it means that we are special and so are all human beings, including our students. Only of the human being did God say "created in our image and likeness." Humans are not the "rational animal" referred to in much scientific literature today, especially in the musings of the social sciences. Instead, humans are placed by God Himself in a qualitatively different category than other living beings, whether the highest animal, angels, or gods (as some other worldviews hold). Adam seemed to need to understand this concept early in his existence. God taught Adam by having him use his God-given mind and language facility to name the animals, probably based on some of their characteristics. I do not know what he named them, nor the language he used. But I do know this from the text: he found none to be like himself as a human. Now he was ready for the surgery that created Eve at the hand of God. When Adam awakened and saw Eve, he called her "woman" (some might even suggest that he said with delight, "Whoa man!"). She was a human and not an animal, one to help in cultivating and enjoying the earth and one to relate to him on a human level in love and companionship.

Write your thoughts that express the implications for education that follow from your understanding of your students as image-bearers. Address at least one implication for each of the eight listed characteristics and any others you may add.

> • Man have a moral responsibility to God.
> They will one day give account to
> God for the life they lived

Return to the template or pegs to frame our writing about human commonalities.

I. Commonalities

    A. Special category of living things

    B. Moral nature (good, bad, neutral)

    C. Actional Nature (passive, active, interactive—mutually opposed views)

    D. Cognitive and behavioral science research

    E. General developmental nature

Moral Nature

"Nature" refers to how we are, naturally, by being born into the human family. Bigge and Shermis (2004) declare: "Innate and basic are synonymous adjectives; both mean 'original' or 'unlearned.'" But they go on to affirm: "there are several distinctly different and mutually opposed answers to this question ['What is the moral nature of human beings?'], each enjoying a good deal of support" (p. 15).

In philosophy and educational theory, there are three basic options that are usually analyzed and then subjected to elaboration or description. The way philosophers address this question about moral nature is to think like this: "Left to themselves without some outside intervention, the human would be _____ bad _____" (good, bad, or neutral).

Different philosophies of education hold different views. The Romantics of the seventeenth century and many humanistic theorists today believe that the human being is born basically good. Behaviorists, however, believe that the human is morally neutral at birth and that the environment makes one good or bad. Freud and other thinkers of the past have held that the human by nature is selfish, aggressive, and yes, bad, perhaps as a result of residual characteristics left over from the animal kingdom from which they evolved. What do Christians usually believe about the moral nature?

Here is a question to ponder from a Christian perspective:

When we use the terms "good," "bad," or "neutral" to describe human nature, who or what is the standard used to measure good or bad when it comes to moral characteristics?

You might ask this question as you read a chapter on Christian Theism such as the one in *The Universe Next Door*. Describing the moral nature will take some thinking and perhaps study on your part. However, the answer to the question is essential. Even secular theorists address this issue:

> Each theory of learning, especially as it applies in schools, is closely linked to a conception of the basic innate moral and actional nature of human beings. Hence, when teachers seriously consider how they are going to teach children and youths, they inevitably formulate some assumptions about the essential moral and actional nature of students as human beings (Bigge and Shermis, p. 14).

Activity | Write: Explain the Human Moral Nature

Your task: Explain the human moral nature from a broad biblical view. Use the biblical story of the human race and the terms, *good, bad,* or *neutral*. Try to define each term and consider the standard for good or bad you are using. You might also use a common biblical, historical framework—Creation, Fall, and Redemption—to state your beliefs. Use Scripture to defend your position.

- The Bible says in Romans 3:10, there is no righteous not one. The Bible tells us man is desperately wicked.

- The Bible gives many examples of man doing that which is right in their own eyes. only evil came of all this.

- Redemption is the reason why christ wants to redeem us. We are helpless without God. we are bad and eternally bound to hell without God because of our wicked sin.

Think like this: How were the first humans created originally: good, bad, or neutral (or what)? What characteristics are inherent in humans as image bearers that lead to choice and responsibility? What happened when humans were given an instruction by a holy, good God and a choice whether to obey it? What is the source of evil in the world, and how can the problem of evil be addressed in the universe? How did God address it? What does God's solution provide for the human in terms of moral character?

Implications for the Moral Nature

The key implication for the moral nature is related to the question of whether humans need moral instruction, guidance, and intervention from outside themselves. Is there a place for character education in schools? Why?

Reflect again upon Pascal's words and what he must have meant when he wrote:

> It is dangerous to show a man too clearly how much he resembles the beast, without at the same time showing him his greatness. It is also dangerous to allow him too clear vision of his greatness without his baseness. It is even more dangerous to leave him in ignorance of both.

Human "greatness," it seems to me, is related to being created in the image of God with the purpose of reflecting that image as God's creatures on this planet. Human baseness is no doubt related to the Fall and the resultant flawed nature that prevents the human from reflecting God's image as He intended. We could not fix ourselves. We could not fulfill the purpose for which we were made—a sad commentary on the human predicament. The Fall made necessary an outside intervention in the person of Jesus Christ, God's Son, who provided redemption through His death and resurrection and is at work recreating His image and the glory from which we have fallen so that we can once again reflect the God of the universe as He intended. "And we, who with unveiled faces all reflect the Lord's glory, are being transformed into his likeness with ever-increasing glory" (2 Corinthians 3:18).

What do you suppose Pascal meant by his last statement: "It is still more dangerous to leave him in ignorance of both"? Write your thoughts here and include your biblically informed beliefs about the moral nature of humans and the implications for education.

- It is important for man to know how God views him and what God's plan are for him.

- It is important to under man were created for great things but not live for himself but rather to Bring glory to God

- Man has moral responsibilities before God. Therefore, one day he will be accountable to Him.

- Man must learn to submit to the authority of God.

- Man needs to understand, He was created for a great purpose.

*If man is not biblically advised about why and how created Him that He will never find meaning and purpose for life

without God's knowledge man are left in darkness, bondage and depravity

7 Commonalities: Actional and Developmental Nature

Take a moment to review once again the template or "pegs" for writing about human commonalities:

I. Commonalities

    A. Special category of living things

    B. Moral nature (good, bad, neutral)

    C. Actional Nature (passive, active, interactive—mutually opposed)

    D. General developmental nature

The *actional* nature is the most difficult to examine in today's educational circles because of the confusion between learning models and instructional methods. The term *actional* is a technical term used in the field of learning theory that presents implications for learning and teaching models. In this section, the difference between models and methods will be clarified.

Educators bring their own worldviews to the study of instructional theory and practice. Within the boundaries of these beliefs, serious educators examine and choose from among the practical options that fit with their worldviews. Confusion may occur as teachers and practitioners read the literature. Here is an example of a well-written paragraph taken from a Phi Delta Kappa Fastback, *Constructivist Teaching*, that may help the reader understand some aspects of decision-making in teaching but may also lead to some confusion in deciding upon applications.

> Deciding about any instructional procedure is a matter of examining possible instructional methods to determine which are consistent with one's beliefs. Research and theory are helpful in identifying ways to teach. But teachers need to decide for themselves which techniques they will and will not use. When reduced to their essential character, these decisions deal with *beliefs about students*, their human qualities and learning processes, and with *beliefs about knowledge*, its form and function. If the beliefs about students and knowledge embedded in the technique or practice match the beliefs the teacher has about the students and knowledge, the technique will be one that fits the teacher (Zahorik 1995, p. 33).

The author goes on to declare that there are just two views of the students and two views of knowledge that are especially important. However, as you will see, there are three.

Two Historical Views

The prevailing two actional descriptors of the nature of the human and learning, *passive* and *active*, describe how the human being relates to the environment in the learning process. These two views have been at war for more than 100 years in American education and, more recently, in other global educational systems as well. Even today, most educational articles address problems in education as being related to passive versus active learning approaches. The authors usually take a strong position toward one or the other, and the war between the two continues without resolution for many. Educational practices tend to swing back and forth between each of these polar views.

Many teachers interpret the terms *passive* and *active* as physical activity and physical passivity, referring to methods rather than to the nature of the human and learning that should inform our overall teaching approach. If you have never studied the actional nature of the human, you may need to do a little bit of research on your own. (It could be that the term *actional* is not one to which you have been exposed, but you may already understand the concept. The concept will be defined below.)

A Third View

Morris Bigge and Samuel Shermis (2004) identify a third view of the actional nature of human beings and learning. That view is labeled "interactive." This view may help to solve the 100-year war between active and passive learning. Bigge and Shermis suggest that the reasons for various interpretations of experimental research in the field of psychology lie in the underlying beliefs related to human nature held by the researcher: "These differences appear to stem from disagreements over the fundamental nature of human beings and their relationship to their environments and the nature of motivation and perception" (p. 45).

To what does the actional nature refer?

Bigge and Shermis use the term *actional* to refer to the nature of the relationship between humans and their environment, as well as to the source of human motivation. Motivation, it is thought, stems from (1) inside, (2) outside, or (3) inside triggered by either inside or outside factors. Those who hold that humans are autonomously active in their actional nature believe that underlying psychological characteristics are inborn; learning comes from forces inside the person. Learning is chiefly developmental. The environment is simply a location for natural unfoldment (the Romantic, humanistic theory tradition). Those who hold that humans are basically passive in their actional nature believe that human characteristics are determined primarily by the environment, forces outside the person (the behavioristic tradition). The human is simply a reactor to the environment. Those who hold the third viewpoint, that the human is interactive in actional nature, do not equate learning with the simple unfoldment of inner patterns or promptings, nor with the conditioning process that works on the human being from without. They believe that psychological characteristics arise as humans take in information from the outside world and try to make sense of it by using their innate capacity to come to know and their prior knowledge (or lack thereof) (Bigge and Shermis, pp. 15–16).

A good treatment of the three possible views of the human "actional" nature may be found in Bigge and Shermis' book *Learning Theories for Teachers*, now published in the *Allyn & Bacon Classics in Education* series.

A Brief Critique

The two historical competing views concerning the nature of the human and learning, passive or active, have arisen somewhat as corollaries to the two broad philosophical camps represented by the Enlightenment and Romanticism. Some would say they are corollaries to the two broad camps, Realism and Idealism. The passive view represents, on the one hand, a scientific, mechanical, deterministic view; a focus on outside factors; and objective knowledge that exists in its own right that can be transmitted, conditioned, discovered through the five senses, and reproduced photographically. On the other hand, the autonomously active view represents a nonscientific perspective that champions personal development, freedom, and choice; a focus on the inside creation of truth; and the unfoldment of organic patterns existing since conception. Although simplified, the two views above are representative of Behaviorism and Humanistic Theory, respectively. I believe that there is a way to reconcile the two, at least in the field of education, by understanding the nature of the human being and learning as neither autonomously active nor passively reactive, but rather as cognitively interactive in actional nature.

Implications Related to the Actional Nature

The primary assumption of the theory that flows out of the view of the human as interactive in actional nature is that something inside the learner and something outside work together *as a unit* in the learning event. This seems like common sense to me.

| **Activity** | **Implications for Learning** |

What are some implications for learning if one understands the interactive nature? Think for a minute of the difference that it might make in teaching in a school classroom if both inner and outer factors held equal importance in the learning event. What might that look like in a lesson or in a classroom in general (classroom management and discipline, for example)?

> The truth is the truth
> • it cannot be changed
> , is eternal.
> if everything is viewed
> through of biblical
> worldview the
> truth will not
> contradict the knowledge
> and reality of facts

> • knowledge and
> reality
> (However "reality"
> if view as subjective
> • can affect the
> classroom try
> may children
> learn).

Cognitive Interactive Learning

Cognitive interactive learning provides a framework for understanding human learning that acknowledges equally inside and outside factors in the learning event and thus in the educational enterprise. This view offers a third approach to present in the 100-year war in education between proponents of the active nature or the passive nature. The pendulum swing between active vs. passive, process vs. content, student-centered vs. subject-centered, and progressive vs. traditional must now take into account a third mutually opposed label—interactive—and its implications for education. While this latter concept has been around in various forms for years, many educators have not, in my opinion, really understood that the interactive label is not just student talk and cooperative learning (these are methods, not "nature"). Nor is it a balance between passive and active (sometimes active, sometimes passive). It is a wholly different and mutually opposed viewpoint.

Early twentieth-century cognitive interactionists reacted against the behavioristic view of human nature as passive, reactive, and nonpurposive. Many used the term *active learning* to describe their opposition. John Dewey and Jerome Bruner were two who did this in their writings. However, close examination of their work indicates elements of the interactive nature without the use of the term itself. Some educational philosophers of the last century sought a balance between inner and outer factors. Lois LeBar declared in the mid-twentieth century:

> Educators in our own day are striving to achieve a balance between inner and outer factors. They realize the inadequacies both of so-called poor traditional education that seemed satisfied if students could parrot back content . . . and of progressive education that seems content to provide experience without sufficient guidance by teachers (LeBar 1958, p. 45).

While LeBar's balanced approach helped teachers such as myself to design curriculum, it also left the door open for teachers to favor one—active (inner student focus) or passive (outer teacher focus)—while paying lip service to the other. There was no overall approach to teaching that could really be described as interactive, based upon a mutually opposing view of the actional nature that would, by definition, exclude favoring one over the other. This is because interactive learning is viewed as including inside and outside factors as a unified whole in the process of learning. Now, many years later, there is an accepted label: *interactive*.

A Word About Constructivism and the Concept of Human Nature as Interactive

Today, the leading theory of learning most written about and studied in schools of education around the world is Constructivism. While most constructivists hold to the interactive nature of the human, they disagree among themselves on the nature of knowledge and reality. These disagreements have led to a strong movement to classify Constructivism outside the cognitive interactive camp as a theory of learning. As such, Constructivism lies on a continuum that moves beyond the interactive actional nature toward the autonomously active actional nature. While giving lip service to the fact that something must be there to reach out to and use for constructions, many Constructivists believe that what is there can never be known as truth in the sense that it corresponds to some external reality. Humans create their own reality. This view must be rejected by one who holds to a Christian worldview. The basic view, described in this book, of the student (human) as interactive varies greatly from Constructivism in its radical form. The basic interactive view treats outside and inside factors as operating together in the learning event and of equal importance. In the radical version of Constructivism, inside factors are far more important, and truth as correspondence to an independent reality is not accepted. There is no affirmation that an external world exists separate from the knower, as Ernst von Glasersfeld suggests in his book *Radical Constructivism:*

> Radical constructivism . . . replaces the notion of 'truth' (as true representation of an independent reality) with the notion of 'viability' within the subjects' experiential world. Consequently, it refuses all metaphysical commitments and claims to be no more than one possible model of thinking about the only world we can come to know, the world we construct as living subjects (1995, p. 22).

An educator evaluating sub-theories of cognitive interactive theory, if informed by a biblical worldview, must consider not only the actional nature of the learner but also the nature of *knowledge* and knowing. This latter issue will be examined briefly in the "Nature and Purpose of the Curriculum" section of this book (chapters 11 and 12). Those who hold to cognitive interactive principles informed by a biblical view disagree with the radical constructivists on the nature of knowledge rather than on the basic view of human nature as interactive. Christians view truth, reality, and knowledge as existing separately from the knower, prior to and external to the knowing mind, even though there is a sure measure of subjectivity in coming to know what is there to be known.

Instructional Philosophy: Overall Approach to Teaching

In developing a philosophy of education, educators must answer certain questions about human nature before committing to an overall approach to teaching. For example: Does the educator believe that the human is a set of matter or material highly organized and determined, but nonpurposive, one that is passive in learning, receiving from the environment objective knowledge as a photograph or exact copy "untouched" by the processing of the human mind? Or does the educator hold that the human is an autonomous chooser who makes his own world, creating his own reality and knowledge? The answers to these worldview questions vary greatly and offer very different suggestions as to how humans learn what they learn. So too, does the answer offered by the third option, the interactive view, a view that might be adopted for various reasons and from divergent sources but one that may fit best with a biblical worldview.

For the person informed by a Christian worldview, one of the three mutually opposed views will emerge from study. Christian philosopher Gordon Clark (1981) describes his answers related to human knowing in a chapter on epistemology in *A Christian View of Men and Things*. He writes, "God has fashioned both the mind and the world so that they harmonize" (p. 316). His view does not suggest that we can know reality perfectly, but it does suggest that a world exists outside the human mind that is knowable by the human mind, for God made them both. Truth (true information that corresponds to an existent reality) can be known, in spite of human limits and human perspectives. The mind (inside factor) has been created with the capacity to learn and come to know what is there to be known (outside factor).

James Emery White shares his beliefs related to this issue when he writes in *A Mind for God*:

> The Christian mind is a mind that operates under the belief that there is something outside of ourselves that we must take into account. There is a God, a God, as Francis Schaeffer said, who is not only there but is not silent (p. 21).

Reason would inform one who holds to a Christian worldview that learning as a process requires inside and outside factors. Furthermore, humans may construe correctly or incorrectly. Humans can be wrong. Ongoing assessment, new information, and opportunities to reorganize and change are vital in learning. The interactive view, with a robust focus on both inside and outside factors, leaves room to preserve the concept that reality/objects exist outside the knowing mind independent of our experiencing them, as philosopher Mortimer Adler avowed in *Ten Philosophical Mistakes* (1985). The philosophical mistake he is addressing in the quotes below is related to the typical epistemology of postmodernism (and, to some extent, radical Constructivism).

Activity   Examine and Evaluate

Underline key ideas in the following quotes that relate to the paragraphs above.
Adler wrote:

> In general it can be said that knowing **is not like eating**. When we eat something, we take it into our bodies, digest it, assimilate it. It becomes part of us. It no longer remains what it was before it was eaten. But with one striking exception, our knowing something in no way affects or alters the thing known. We may take it into our minds in some way, but doing that leaves it exactly the same as it was before we knew it ...

The knowledge should bring change

There is a sense in which knowing **is like eating**. The edible, before it is eaten, exists quite independently of the eater and is whatever it is regardless of how it is transformed by being eaten. So, too, the knowable exists quite independently of the knower and is whatever it is whether it is known or not, and however it is known.

The word most of us use to signify the independent character of the knowable is the word 'reality.' If there were no reality, nothing the existence and character of which is independent of the knowing mind, there would be nothing knowable. Reality is that which exists whether we think about it or not, and has the character that it has no matter how we think about it.

The reality that is knowable may or may not be physical. It may or may not consist solely of things perceptible to our senses. But whatever its character, its existence must be public, not private. It must be knowable by two or more persons. Nothing that is knowable by one person alone can have the status of knowledge (1985, pp. 88–89).

Write your thoughts here or discuss the quote with a colleague or partner.

Knowledge - needs to become acknowledge by the knower
in order to be knowledge
whether a person accepts it or not
Truth is true whether a person
accepts it or not.

The interactive view of human nature champions, in addition to the existence of an outside reality and external knowledge, the concept that the human innate capacity for processing and developing meanings and understandings is an essential element in learning. Inside and outside factors matter! Understanding the concept of the interactive learner is the starting point for the development of pedagogical (teaching) implications. Students do not all *get it* exactly as the teacher presents it. Assessment is vital.

Pause and do a bit of research from the teaching ministry of Jesus. Find at least five teaching incidents in His teaching ministry with the disciples that you can use to defend the concept that both inside factors (the capacity to process information using prior knowledge or lack thereof, the use of language and vocabulary, and specific knowledge base) and outside factors (spoken truth, illustrations, writings, examples in stories, and parables, etc.) work together in learning. Be ready to write a summary of your findings and a conclusion. If you are working through this book as an exercise in thinking through your own philosophy, it would be prudent to do this exercise before reading the examples given on the following pages.

- Jesus in his teachings had many object lessons that were known by His audience which He used to teach the truth or get His message across. Parable of the seed the sower

- He used already familiar objects to teach a truth.

  - The vine and branches
  - The sower.
  - The prodical son

Here are two examples. Did you find five others?

Example #1

In the teaching ministry of Jesus, one may readily see His expectations related to the inside processing of information and the receptivity of His teachings that are coming from outside the learner. On one occasion a lawyer, wishing to trap Jesus, asked Him about eternal life. Jesus questioned the lawyer about his current knowledge of the law (Luke 10). The student gave the right response: "Love the Lord your God with all your heart and with all your soul and with all your strength and with all your mind; and love your neighbor as yourself." Jesus replied, "You have answered correctly. Do this and you will live." Not satisfied and wishing to justify himself, the student asked, "Who is my neighbor?" Jesus did not lecture the answer, but He did tell a story about a good Samaritan. After the story, He asked the lawyer-student which of the three in the story he thought was neighbor of the man in need. The student processed and answered his own question by replying to the story and the Teacher's question, "The one who had mercy on him." In this learning event, the Teacher was saying, "I'll give you some information (the story), but you need to process it and draw a conclusion!" His overall approach is interactive. He challenged the mind (inside) with outside information and questions. On this occasion Jesus used several methods: questioning, storytelling, listen-to-find-out, direct instruction from outside, and processing from the story and prior knowledge (the student already knew the scriptural command to love his neighbor). These were used to activate inside processing and the drawing of conclusions.

Example # 2

On another occasion, Jesus asked His disciples the question: "Who do people say that I am?" (Matthew 16; Mark 8, Luke 9). The disciples responded that some believed He was John the Baptist, Elijah, or some other prophet. Jesus asked, "Who do you say I am?" Peter, speaking perhaps for the group, declared, "You are the Christ." Now, Jesus knew that the answer given by the stimulus-response (Stimulus: "Who am I?" Response: "The Christ") was the right answer; however, He also knew that Peter did not have complete understanding. The teacher, Jesus, arranged a field trip several days later. He took Peter, James, and John to the Mount of Transfiguration (Matthew 17:2) where God the Father allowed Moses and Elijah to appear with Jesus before the three disciples. Now Peter, who had incomplete understanding in his thinking and was frightened, spoke, "If you wish, I will put up three shelters—one for you (Jesus), one for Moses and one for Elijah." Peter, the student, revealed a misconception or incomplete understanding through his communication. He did not understand that Jesus was the Christ, the Son of God and in a different category than the others (fully God and fully man—not simply a man, like Moses and Elijah). God the Father covered over Moses and Elijah, and Jesus appeared in His glorified form alone. God the Father (the teacher in this learning event) spoke (direct instruction) and said, "This is my Son…Listen to him." Now, human teachers could not do what God did in this instance in their classrooms! But we can use the interactive principle to encourage learning and to encourage communication (writing or, as in Peter's case, speaking) in order to assess understandings. Both inner and outer factors were considered as both impressive methods (seeing and listening; they saw Christ and Moses and Elijah and listened to the voice of the Father) and expressive methods (Peter/student talking) were used to promote thinking and learning.

Questions: Why did Jesus teach His disciples in the way He did?
What can we conclude from the examples of His teaching ministry?

o Man can be rational in their thinking.

• Jesus maynt menn to think critically and form their own belueves based facts and true,

• Jesus used the known information

Jesus was always concerned with the inside processing of the student as well as with the truth to which He was referring. He often used the prior knowledge and experiences of the student to get the mind actively processing what He was saying. He was also concerned about development and readiness to learn. He did not ask, "Who do men say that I am?" until many months after He began His ministry with the disciples. The disciples needed more experience. When they were ready, He presented and facilitated new information.

Many years ago in my first college teaching experience, I was about three weeks into a class on children's ministry, required of all students in the five available programs. Out of 40 students, about 10 were pastoral majors. One of these young sophomore pastoral students, leaning back in his chair as though he was sure he did not need to learn about children, commented at the end of class that "gimmicks" (his word) and methods were not needed unless there was something wrong with the message or the messenger! I invited him to stay after class for a brief chat and an assignment. I asked him to choose 10 of Christ's teaching incidents directed toward his disciples and examine them carefully in terms of the student and the teacher and then draw any conclusions he could (I had to do this in one of my graduate classes at Wheaton College with far more than 10). The student was to report his findings to the next class as a substitute assignment for what the rest of the class was doing related to methods. In his report, he began this way: "There was nothing wrong with Jesus as a teacher and nothing wrong with his message! However, he used methods in his teaching." He went on to describe what he had found in the 10 incidents. Then he shared his conclusion: "I have discovered, I think, that Jesus used methods because He knew how humans learn because He is our creator. His 'lesson' design was not to use gimmicks or methods for the sake of creativity or to disguise a weak message, but rather to get the student thinking and deciding." Bingo! A powerful lesson learned.

| Activity | Continued Research |

What incidents in the teaching ministry of Christ with His disciples did you find? Share those with others or jot them here.

Jesus asked them questions
let them to think
ask them to meditate
To ponder in the true

o Jesus led his disciples to come to
a conclusion.

While it is recognized that the Bible is not a learning theory textbook, it does portray, by precept and example, a clear picture of the human that helps one to select the interactive actional nature as most closely aligning with a biblical view of human nature and learning. It is a view that can also preserve truth that exists outside the knowing mind.

8 | Implications: The Actional Nature

A Common Misconception

An educator who has not understood the concept of the *interactive* (actional) psychological nature of the student and learning might speak like this: "Well, sometimes students are passive when I am talking and they are listening, and other times they are active when they are doing something or talking to one another. Don't you think they can be both passive and active?" The answer is no. This confused teacher is referring to methods that promote physical activity or passivity rather than referring to the way the mind works in the learning event. The term *interactive* connotes more than a mix or balance between passive and active methods. It is indeed a term that connotes how the human mind works in the learning event even during a lecture. Standards for knowledge, and therefore feedback assessment, as well as concern for how the human is conceptualizing, understanding, and making sense of the information are all important and will require various methods in interactive learning!

Developing a Teaching Model Based on an Understanding of the Nature of the Learner

Three examples from passive, active, and interactive theories:

Behaviorism

Behaviorism, the instructional theory that dominated much of the twentieth century and is alive and well today, holds that the human actional nature is passive and that learning happens because of outside factors (i.e., the teacher, the textbook, the DVD, the Internet, the reinforcers). The learning model derived from this belief focuses on outside stimuli soliciting a response or reaction. Future responses (learning) are determined by the skilled conditioner-teacher's reinforcement. Outside forces trump anything inside the learner. The model for teaching is very teacher-centered. Methods for teaching are primarily impressive or based on input.

Even after the cognitive revolution had taken hold in America, behaviorist B. F. Skinner never changed his mind. When interviewed by Daniel Goleman for the *New York Times* in 1987, Skinner's response to an inquiry related to new cognitive information processing theories was to declare, "The cognitive revolution is a search inside the mind for something that is not there. You can't see yourself process information. Information processing in an inference from behavior and a bad one at that" (Goleman 1987). Skinner's stimulus-response approach to learning leads to an overall teaching model that became: "*teacher* tells; *teacher* expects students to take notes exactly as given; *teacher* tests expecting exact answers as given in the notes; *teacher* reinforces (after the test or quiz)."

Humanistic Theory

Current-day Humanistic theorists have adopted much from the views of the eighteenth century Romantic Naturalists, the Neo-Romantics, Existential Humanists of the 1960s, and some current-day postmodernist thought. These theorists believe that the human actional nature is autonomously active and that learning occurs primarily because of inside factors naturally unfolding. Learning is autonomous and developmental. Inside factors trump anything outside. The model for teaching is student-centered. Methods for teaching are primarily expressive. Friedrich Froebel (1887/1906), Father of the Kindergarten, held the belief that, "All the child is ever to be and become lies . . . in the child, and can be attained only through development from within outward." He went on to say, "The purpose of teaching and instruction is to bring ever more *out* of man rather than to put more and more *into* him." Froebel held that humans unfold like a flower. Thus, a teaching approach for Unfoldment (Humanistic) Theory might look like this: activity, activity, activity designed to draw out what is already there. *Student* interest and needs guide activities as the child unfolds; *students* learn through their own prompting; *student* activities involve the student in the self-direction of their own learning and development; *student* enjoyment and fun are the focus; feelings and emotions are central; *students* are naturally motivated. There is no need to plan for motivation; classroom environment is simply a location for *student* activity.

Implications for the active and passive views are summarized in the following chart.

	Active	**Passive**
Relation to Environment	Underlying human characteristics are inborn. Environment is merely a location for unfoldment of what is within. Motivation is solely from within.	Human characteristics are primarily products of the environment. Behaviors are the result of outside forces. Humans are nonpurposive. Motivation must come from outside in the form of reinforcement.
Proponents	Rousseau, Pestalozzi, Froebel, Maslow	Skinner, Thorndike, Watson
Teaching Model	Draw out— Activity, activity, activity with the focus on the enjoyment of thinking and doing	Put in— Tell, explain, test, reinforce (grade) with the focus often on the reinforcer, the grade

No wonder the competing theories of learning at war for over 100 years have been called "teacher/content-centered" vs. "child/student centered"! Conversations in the teachers' lounge between teachers who hold the two competing views might go something like this:

Teacher One: "Well, my goal is to teach children. I teach kids!"

Teacher Two: "What do you teach them?"

Teacher One: "I teach them to think!"

Teacher Two: "Think about what?"

Teacher One: "Well, they are learning to learn."

Teacher Two: "Learning what? Look, if you elementary teachers taught kids concepts, rules, and skills, the basics of geography, the framework for interpreting history, the basic generalizations of science, and interrelated patterns and relationships in math, we middle school and high school teachers would not have to go all the way back to ground zero in our subjects when you send the kids to us!"

Teacher One: "Maybe so, but if our focus was like yours—content, content, content—we would be delivering to you a bunch of academic clones and psychologically stressed students! Kids are individuals. Personal development and human creativity are the primary goals of education."

And the war goes on. Do you hear any of your colleagues or classmates in the conversation above? A cognitive interactive approach would add a third dimension to the conversation above and would offer a possible resolution. Could you complete the chart and write into the conversation in the teachers' lounge a third point of view? Write your thoughts here:

	Active	Passive	Interactive
Relation to Environment	Underlying human characteristics are inborn. Environment is merely a location for unfoldment of what is within. Motivation is solely from within.	Human characteristics are primarily products of the environment. Behaviors are the result of outside forces. Humans are nonpurposive. "Motivation" must come from outside in the form of reinforcement.	• ask questions let children think • Think critically rationally • use the info they know to
Proponents	Rousseau, Pestalozzi, Froebel, Maslow	Skinner, Thorndike, Watson	My reality is not your reality
Teaching Model	Draw out— Activity, activity, activity with the focus on the enjoyment of thinking and doing	Put in— Tell, explain, test, reinforce (grade) with the focus often on the reinforcer, the grade	"you can draw your own conclusions

Interactive Model

The model for teaching that emerges when one considers the interactive nature might be as follows:

If something inside matters in the learning of new information, I must plan to engage that inside something in order to activate prior knowledge and motivate toward learning the lesson at hand.

- **If something outside matters,** I must study and organize content and skill development strategies to deliver these in light of the students' prior experiences, current skill level, and knowledge base.

- **If learning occurs as information is taken in and processed by the individual,** I must create student processing activities, both group and individual, that are designed to help the student fit in, make sense of new information, construct adequate understandings, and practice skills.

- **If learning occurs inside as a student processes new information and skills and develops understandings and meanings, and if I am a teacher who must assess learning** to see how well the student has understood, connected, and made sense of the material and can use it, then I must create ongoing assessment activities that provide feedback, answering the teacher's question, "Are they getting it?" and the students' question, "Am I getting it?"

Something inside, yes, and something outside (the criteria or standard for the knowledge gained) are both vital.

A teaching model based upon the interactive nature of the human and learning is not just passive telling and testing. Nor is it unguided activity, activity, activity—simply drawing out. Rather, it is an orchestration of four basic elements (not necessarily steps).

1. **Engaging the mind** (inside) toward the lesson at hand by using an activity planned by the teacher (outside). I call this a "motivation" element in the lesson plan. The teacher plans to activate the inside motivation for learning in the student. Motivation has directionality. It can be toward or away from something, and the teacher's role is to activate it in the direction of the lesson at hand. While attention is needed, motivation involves far more than physical attention.

2. **Providing new information** (outside the student) by giving it or creating a student activity that requires the student to get new information from an outside source (textbook, original document, DVD, Internet, labs, etc.).

3. **Creating student processing activities** (outside and inside) to help the student make sense out of new material or skills, to form closure (fit it in), make connections (with prior knowledge), generalize, draw conclusions, or practice and use a skill.

4. **Assessing learning** (inside) by using student expressions of constructed understandings as feedback on whether students are "getting it" or can perform a developing skill.

Activity | Evaluating the Interactive Approach

Look at the above four elements and determine why each element really matters in this approach to learning.

- Why is subject matter (content) vital?

  It creates a foundation for teaching.

- Why does the notion of outside information matter?

  We can draw and study facts

- Why is the prior knowledge of the learner and his or her knowledge base important?

  His experience, His understanding.

- Why are student processing activities not an option, but rather a requirement in this model?

  It creates students to actively involved

- Why is memory (storage) essential in this model?

  helps children know where they stand

- Why are remembering and understanding keys to learning and transfer? (Transfer of learning is the ability to retrieve and use the information in various settings to solve problems, make decisions, and appreciate and grow with new knowledge and experiences.)

  we can use facts and think clearly and make rational decision

- Why is assessment vital?

  Review, responding to learned info.

Methodology in the interactive learning/teaching model always includes both impressive (listening and reading) and expressive activities (speaking and writing) in every lesson because of the interactive nature of the learner. The term *interactive* is sometimes misconstrued by my students before they study the actional nature. Interactive is thought of as simply social interaction (talk). Ask any group of teachers to identify which of these methods below fit with their idea of interactive learning:

1) Cooperative learning groups using project and discussion methods

2) Class discussion where all are involved together

3) Some time for questions planned into the lesson

4) Technology in the classroom

Most will say that all of them fit the concept of interactive learning. They see interactive learning as primarily "social interaction" or talking. This is a misconception! These are methods—good ones—but still methods. Interactive learning can occur even in a lecture to 500 people. It refers to how the mind works in the learning event.

In cognitive interactive learning, the strengths of both content-centered and student-centered approaches are recognized and integrated into a more robust approach that seems to fit the way God intended humans to learn. Teachers who are serious about promoting learning in their students will invite conversation about the potential of approaches that are built upon the interactive nature of humans. Advocates see learning as a unified process involving content and experience, knowing and doing, and information for change. Learning is transformational.

We can now fill in the rest of this chart and compare it to your previous work.

	Active	**Passive**	**Interactive**
Relation to Environment	Underlying human characteristics are inborn. Environment is merely a location for unfoldment of what is within. Motivation is solely from within.	Human characteristics are primarily products of the environment. Behaviors are the result of outside forces. Humans are nonpurposive. "Motivation" must come from outside in the form of reinforcement.	Human characteristics result from the person making sense of the physical and social environment. Person-environment is a reciprocal relationship. Motivation may be a reciprocal process. Inside is often triggered by outside factors.
Proponents	Rousseau, Pestalozzi, Froebel, Maslow	Skinner, Thorndike, Watson	Dewey, Tolman, Vygotsky, Bruner, Bandura, Bigge and Shermis; Developmentalists such as Piaget
Teaching Model	Draw out— Activity, activity, activity with the focus on the enjoyment of thinking and doing	Put in— Tell, explain, test, reinforce (grade) with the focus often on the reinforcer, the grade	Engage the mind— Provide (make available) new information through exploration and explanation Student Processing activities and construction of meaning and understanding Ongoing assessment (MacCullough)

Where does your current thinking fit with the viewpoints concerning the actional human nature? Have you been a cheerleader for content as the primary focus of teaching? Have you been a crusader for student activity and processing? How has your thinking been clarified, supported, or changed as you have read the last two chapters? Write a brief reflection on the concept of the actional nature and implications for learning. This will help you begin to write the section on "commonalities." Add the actional nature to the first two categories already addressed: (1) humans are in a special category of living beings, and (2) they have a moral nature that must be considered in an educational philosophy.

Reflections of your changing or modified beliefs:

- It is essential to always view children the God sees them.

- To understand our students we must understand the way God created them and for what purpose

- Interactive nature is could be of a great help in Christian ed

mind/information
  ↳ student processing activity, access
  activities = impression →
            expressive

S
M
A
G

9 | Human Differences

Before examining what one believes about human differences, it is necessary to review one category of human commonality that fits under both categories in the template we are using. The final peg upon which to hang our thoughts in examining the commonalities of humans and learning is related to the developmental nature of humans as living beings.

I. Commonalities

    A. Special category of living things

    B. Moral nature (good, bad, neutral)

    C. Actional Nature (passive, active, interactive—mutually opposed)

    D. General developmental nature | *commonalities*

At some point in your education, you may have studied human developmental characteristics, especially of school-aged children and you may have charted the averages by ages or grade level using social, physical, mental, and emotional categories. The commonality related to developmental characteristics is simply the fact that humans are indeed developmental by nature. We all start out as babies—6–9 pounds and 20 inches in length, on average—and we grow. We experience both limits and potentials in several categories of development as organic patterns unfold over time in a context that helps or hinders growth. Humans mature by nature, and, while human development is not the same as learning, it is certainly related. In fact, most teachers have heard over and over again the necessity of using developmentally appropriate methods. Bigge and Shermis (2004) state the commonality this way: "Lasting changes in persons occur within the processes of maturation, learning, or a combination of the two" (p. 1).

All learners are growing developing.

• learning produces change and maturation

> **Maturation** is a developmental process within which a person from time to time manifests traits whose 'blueprints' have been carried in the person's cells from the time of conception. *displaying the traits already possessed at Birth*
>
> **Learning**, in contrast with maturation, is an enduring change in a living individual that is not heralded by genetic inheritance.
>
> —Bigge and Shermis, *Learning Theories for Teachers*, p. 1

Activity   Read and Draw a Conclusion

Read the following verses and see if you can draw a conclusion that might help you word your beliefs about human development.

Luke 2:52

"And Jesus grew in wisdom and in stature, and in favor with God and men." (It seems self-evident that Mary had a baby and He was not born the size of a man. Physical development is the easiest to "see.") *Christ growing in wisdom which is learning and in stature would be physical development.*

1 Corinthians 13:11

"When I was a child, I talked like a child; I thought like a child, I reasoned like a child. When I became a man, I put childish ways behind me." *This verse describes the physical developmental process within a person*

Proverbs 22:6

"Train a child in the way he should go, and when he is old he will not turn from it."

Hebrews 6:1a, 3

"Therefore let us leave the elementary teachings about Christ and go on to maturity.... And God permitting, we will do so." (The concept of maturing spiritually using development as an illustration.) *This verse speaks of growing in wisdom, mental, spiritual*

You may wish to add several other passages to help defend the concept that humans are developmental by nature. This is a concept that most educators and psychologists accept today but one that was not addressed clearly in descriptions about teaching and learning until the field of psychology began to champion the idea in the nineteenth century. As well, Behaviorism did not sufficiently address the issue. It is worthwhile to address the concept of human development as a part of your philosophy (if you are indeed convinced that it is a vital issue related to learning).

human development part of philosophy.

Write at least one implication for the general concept of development.

It involves individual and always creates change in an individual. May be physical, mental, spiritual and social growth. It is limited to one type of development.

Critical thinking: evaluates and judges against a standard.

Human Differences

Returning to the template for examining beliefs related to the nature of the student and learning, we now address differences, beginning with developmental differences.

Template for writing about the nature of the human and learning

I. Commonalities *general / categorize*
   A. Special Category of living things (Why special?)
   B. Moral nature (good, bad, neutral)
   C. Actional Nature (passive, active, interactive—these are mutually opposed)
   D. General developmental nature *, changing*

   common

II. Differences (Human differences by birth or developed over time, individual, and cultural)
   A. **Individual developmental variance from the norm (statistical curve)** *different rates, highs etc*
   variance of development
   B. Individual preferences and capacities in learning—brain or experience related—learning styles, multiple intelligences, cognitive processing, for example *preferences & capacities.*
   C. Cultural and social forces that affect individuals and groups of individuals
   D. Various other abilities and disabilities *dislexia* *[people photographic memory.*

One of the most common statements made by current teachers or teachers-to-be is that they must consider human diversity and adjust their teaching to human differences. Differentiated learning is a basic topic in most schools of education today. In this section, we examine the underlying beliefs concerning individuality that fit with a biblical worldview and thus serve to inform a Christian's philosophy of education.

Individual Developmental Variance from the Norm

Why start with developmental variance? Did we not address human development under commonalities? Correct! We did address the concept that human beings are developmental by nature. However, one mistake new teachers often make is to take those human developmental characteristics charted in education classes in college and think that all second graders are pretty much like the general average developmental characteristics on their chart and therefore the lesson plan should be targeted in that direction. Remember that the general developmental characteristics observed by researchers are averages! (Therefore, there must be students who fall above and below the average.) ⚹

Activity | Take a Little Quiz

As a teacher...

Do you teach to the middle? Why, or why not?

I do not know what this is implying

Do you treat children the same regardless of developmental differences (equally) or differently in light of developmental differences (fairly)? Why?

Treat children equally despite differences

Do all children process your lessons and learn in exactly the same way? Why, or why not?

Not all children will. Some struggle with concepts or ability to grasp them faster.

Are all the children in one classroom at the same developmental level? Why did you answer as you did?

Not all the children will process a lesson the same equally

Discuss your answers with another person or write your answers here.

All are different from one another

Do you view a class of students as a group, as individuals, or something else?

fearfully and wonderfully made

Study the following pairs of biblical characters—real people—and determine their similarities and differences. This can be done by one individual studying all eight characters or in pairs or small groups, each taking a biblical pair and then sharing conclusions.

Moses	Daniel	Deborah	Peter
Aaron	David	Barak	Paul

- "Read out" or "think out" individual differences. List these.

- Which one of your pair would you rather have in class? Why?

- How might you need to differentiate or accommodate for each one in the pair?

- Draw a conclusion about God's perspective on individual differences. What (if anything) can you conclude from this brief study? Be ready to add your conclusions to your developing document.

Write your study thoughts here:

peter and paul are 2 different individuals
Have a family background education history

Children can have a love for truth
Children are capable of learning

How can you apply to teachers?

Returning to the template:

Moving to the second peg in the template for examining beliefs related to the nature of the student and learning, we will address individual preferences and capacities.

II. Differences (Human differences by birth or developed over time, individual, and cultural)

A. Individual developmental variance from the norm (statistical curve)

B. **Individual preferences and capacities in learning—brain or experience related—learning styles, multiple intelligences, cognitive processing, for example**

C. Cultural and social forces that affect individuals and groups of individuals

D. Various other abilities and disabilities

Humans have individual preferences and capacities that impact teaching and learning: cognitive processing skills and memory, learning styles, multiple intelligences (that is, ways of expressing intelligence), learning disabilities, multiple challenges of special needs children—physically, mentally, socially, and behaviorally—and the challenges of gifted students. All of these demand an examination by teachers. What do you believe and why; how are these differences addressed (if they are) in a classroom of children under your leadership?

When writing your philosophy of education, you do not need to write about every one of the above, but you do need to write your perspective in dealing with differences. Write only about those issues with which you are familiar and decide what God's perspective might be.

Activity	Further Study

To help in the discovery of a biblical perspective, study the following in addition to the pairs studied previously in the above research activity.

- David and the physically impaired Mephibosheth (2 Samuel 9)
- Queen Esther and her beauty (book of Esther)
- Daniel's giftedness (Daniel 1)
- You may wish to find others

Write your thoughts here:

Cultural and Social Differences

Moving to the third peg in the template for examining beliefs related to the nature of the student and learning, we address the cultural and social forces that affect individuals and groups.

II. Differences (Human differences by birth or developed over time, individual, and cultural)

    A. Individual developmental variance from the norm (statistical curve)

    B. Individual preferences and capacities in learning—brain or experience related—learning styles, multiple intelligences, cognitive processing, for example

    C. Cultural and social forces that affect individuals and groups of individuals

    D. Various other abilities and disabilities

Activity | **Compare the Two People Described Below**

Person #1	Person #2
• Mother and father died when he was a young teen	• Mother died when he was ten
• Wild youth	• Quiet and fairly refined youth
• Lived in poverty in England	• Lived in affluence in Ireland
• Attended the local free school in England	• Attended the best private school in England
• Had no books of his own until marriage; then he had two books and a Bible	• Surrounded by books from every period of time

So far, which one would you rather have in class and why?

different students
· different personalities
God given talents and abilities.

Person #1	Person #2
• Converted to Christ in his mid-20s	• Converted to Christianity in his 30s
• Lived for 60 years	• Lived for 64 years
• Vocation: a tinker who repaired pots and later a preacher	• Vocation: college professor and author

Have you changed your mind?

Person #1	Person #2
• Academic activities: wrote 58 books • Best known work: *Pilgrim's Progress: From This World to That Which Is to Come*	• Academic activities: Wrote more than three dozen books • Wrote: *Pilgrim's Regress: An Allegorical Apology for Christianity, Reason, and Romanticism*

Have you guessed who they are? *Person #1 is John Bunyan and Person #2 is C. S. Lewis.*

Which of the two men would you have predicted to be used by God, and why? What was actually the case? Draw a conclusion about socioeconomic and cultural factors.

You might wish to also make a study of these factors in the Scriptures. For example: Gideon, a poor farmer without a military education, was asked to lead the military against the Midianites. The apostle Paul, with a top-notch education under a well-known teacher, can be contrasted with Peter, a fisherman. Refer to the pairs study done earlier and draw several conclusions. It is God's business to use each of us with the potentials and limits we possess. It is our business as teachers to teach each student in such a way that we maximize potential and minimize limits.

#1 person would be some in class "opportunity to influence

• His life can turn around

The background of a child does not nothing to do with what God can do in their lives.

In addition to social forces, cultural forces affect individuals or groups as well. Several years ago, one of my students took a job teaching a class of fifth grade boys on a Native American reservation in the American Southwest. Three or four weeks after the beginning of the school year, she called to tell me what happened in a mathematics class. When she had taught the mathematics concept the day before, there was good evidence that all 11 boys understood. The next day she called on one of the students to answer a question that she thought could easily be answered by all. The student replied, "I don't know." She went on to ask each boy until half of the class had been asked. Each one answered her, "I don't know." She was puzzled. She knew that some of these boys had to know the answer to her simple question. Later, in the teacher's lounge, she shared her experience with her colleagues who laughed and said, "You just experienced a lesson in cultural differences. If one boy says he does not know the answer, the rest will say that they, too, do not know the answer in order to help their classmate 'save face.'" This former student of mine had just completed her student teaching in a school system outside of Philadelphia, Pennsylvania. When she asked a question there and someone did not know the answer, many hands went up to give the answer. Saving face was not an issue in the northeast region of the country. Cultural differences matter! Teachers must be willing to study and understand the cultural backgrounds of the students.

Activity | Write

Now write what you believe about individual differences and add any other issues of which you are aware related to abilities and disabilities (physical, mental, etc.).

Begin this way: "I believe that humans possess individual differences in _learning capacity_, _social_ , _cultural_ ; therefore I will (or I will not) _generalize_ ."

What are the implications for your beliefs?

10 | The Role of the Teacher

Teachers Are Human, Too

Years ago, I read a story in child psychologist Haim Ginott's book *Teacher and Child*. It was an account of a young boy's view of his teachers:

> Funny about teachers. It's hard to think of them as people. Sometimes when you see them after school and they talk to you personally, you're surprised—because they talk like human beings. But in class they walk around like robots, waiting for you to do something bad so they can yell at you. Except for Mrs. D. . . She is a person even when she is a teacher (p. 119).

While the story is a cute account of a child's perception of teachers, it also speaks about human nature. Are teachers really human, even when they are teaching? All of them or just some, like Mrs. D.? The story also highlights the child's perception of the **role of the teacher** as one who robotically walks around the room waiting for kids to do something bad so she can yell at them. I assume that Mrs. D. smiles and chats and acts more like a human than a robot!

Believe it or not, teachers are human, too. All of them! Therefore, there is no need to rehearse the commonalities and differences related to human nature. However, it would serve administrators well to write their philosophy with the understanding that teachers are human beings and possess all the commonalities of their students, even the factor of development. A seasoned teacher with a family "out of the nest" has a different set of circumstances and is at a developmentally different place than a first-year teacher who is single and right out of college or one who is married and has a young family. Teachers also vary greatly in ability, creativity, cultural background, organizational skills, and professional development. In short, they are diverse! Administrators must understand the humanness of their teaching staff.

Determining the Teacher's Role

Since teachers are human too, there is no reason to write the beliefs about human nature again; however, the focus in a philosophy of school education is on the role of the teacher in the teaching/learning event. How might the two broad camps in pop educational culture (traditional and progressive) describe the role of the teacher? Try to determine what each view might say. Then, after some reflection, write your own beliefs and complete the chart below.

| Activity | Role of the Teacher in the Learning Event |

How would the different philosophies see the role of the teacher?

Traditionalists	Progressives	Your Own Beliefs
Teacher: source of info and authority in classroom knowledge absorbed through lecture o class runs on general standard		

Possible answers will be found below.

Reflection prompts to help you complete the chart:

• What do you think is the most important role of a teacher in a school setting? Why?

• In addition to the most important role, list other roles that you think are important in the teaching profession.

Compare your views to those of the two prominent pop culture educational philosophies. Views of the teacher's role vary between traditional and progressive:

Traditionalists	Progressives
• Authority/boss • Central figure • Dispenser of knowledge • Example	• Friend/guide • Not central figure • Facilitator of learning • Fellow learner

Activity   Read and Describe

Now look at several passages from the Bible that describe the roles of teachers (including parents and leaders). Determine what the role or roles addressed in the verses might be and write the role under the reference. Find any other verses you wish to add and then take all of the roles and create several categories to use for your analysis of the teacher's role in education.

Directions: Read the brief passages and make a list of descriptive terms that express the biblical role and qualities of a teacher.

Deuteronomy 6:5–9

Love the LORD your God with all your heart and with all your soul and with all your strength. These commandments that I give you today are to be upon your hearts. Impress them on your children. Talk about them when you sit at home and when you walk along the road, when you lie down and when you get up. Tie them as symbols on your hands and bind them on your foreheads. Write them on the doorframes of your houses and on your gates.

_____   _____

_____   _____

_____   _____

1 Corinthians 11:1

Follow my example, as I follow the example of Christ.

_____   _____

_____   _____

_____   _____

2 Corinthians 10:8

For even if I boast somewhat freely about the authority the Lord gave us for building you up rather than pulling you down, I will not be ashamed of it.

_____   _____

_____   _____

_____   _____

1 Thessalonians 2:7–8

But we were gentle among you, like a mother caring for her little children. We loved you . . . we were delighted to share . . . our lives.

_____   _____

_____   _____

_____   _____

1 Thessalonians 2:11–12

For you know that we dealt with each of you as a father deals with his own children, encouraging, comforting and urging you to live lives worthy of God, who calls you into his kingdom and glory.

_____   _____

_____   _____

_____   _____

Mark 10:42–45

Jesus called them together and said, "You know that those who are regarded as rulers of the Gentiles lord it over them, and their high officials exercise authority over them. Not so with you. Instead, whoever wants to become great among you must be your servant, and whoever wants to be first must be slave of all. For even the Son of Man did not come to be served, but to serve, and to give his life as a ransom for many."

_____   _____

_____   _____

_____   _____

Jesus saves

1 Peter 5:2–3

Be shepherds of God's flock that is under your care, serving as overseers—not because you must, but because you are willing, as God wants you to be; not greedy for money, but eager to serve; not lording it over those entrusted to you, but being examples to the flock.

_____   _____

_____   _____

_____   _____

Luke 6:40

A student is not above his teacher, but everyone who is fully trained will be like his teacher.

_____   _____

_____   _____

_____   _____

Write a brief paragraph in which you describe beliefs about the teacher's role from a biblical perspective. Compare this paragraph to your original ideas expressed previously on the chart above and to the commonly held beliefs of traditional and progressive philosophies. Draw several conclusions about the roles of the teacher from this brief study.

_____

_____

_____

_____

Although there are numerous ways to categorize the roles for the teacher/leader from a biblical perspective, the following will be used here:

To teach

To serve

To be in charge

To be a role model

Activity | Analyze Your Beliefs

In keeping with the task of developing a philosophy of education, analyze your beliefs related to these and any other categories you have selected by writing your current thinking on each:

To teach—I believe that

To serve means that

To be in charge means that the teacher

To be a role model means that

Add any other category here:

What do you think?

Imagine you were being interviewed for a position in a school and the administrator asked the question, *"What do your think is the most important role of the teacher in a school?"*

What would you say, and why?

The Teacher's Role Is to Teach So That Students Learn

When I ask my students the question, "What do you think is the most important role of the teacher in a school?" invariably I hear some of the following among many other responses: "to love children," "to help them grow up," "to be an example," "to contribute to their lives," etc. While all of these and more are very important, a teacher is hired primarily **to teach, that is, to promote student learning**. It was suggested many years ago by one of the first theorists to hold an interactive view of the human and learning that, in order to fulfill this primary role, a teacher must...

- Know the subject and how it should be learned¹ (nature or structure of the subject matter) *how learning happens in students*

- Know the students and how they learn (nature of human learning)

- Be able to bring the two together to create and deliver lessons that promote learning (development of the curriculum) *How to teach subject.*

(This is my personal summary of the ideas in Jerome Bruner's *Process of Education*.)

Interestingly, you can find all of these elements in Deuteronomy 6. To teach, one must . . .

Know your subject and how it should be learned:

Notice that in that passage the teacher/parent is instructed that "these commandments that I give you today are to be upon your hearts." There is content to learning, and the teacher must know it! In the Old Testament, heart and mind are used somewhat interchangeably. The Deuteronomy passage uses the command, "Love the Lord your God with all heart, with all your soul, and with all your strength," and in the New Testament, this Old Testament verse was quoted by Jesus (Mark 12:29) as, "Love the Lord your God with all your heart and with all your soul and with all your mind and with all your strength." Again in Luke 10:27, "Love the Lord with all your mind," is included. It is apparent from the Scriptures that the teacher must have a cognitive grasp of the subject, that is, must know the content to be taught. Further, the content must have been processed, understood, and internalized with a heart commitment toward using it.

As the dean of Cairn University's School of Education, I often interviewed prospective students who wished to be enrolled in teacher preparation programs.

I asked them why they wanted to enter the field of education. I was not surprised to hear them say, "Because I love children." My response was to ask, "Do you love to study?" Surprisingly, some replied, "Not really!" I asked, "Do you like mathematics?" And a few of the students wishing to teach at the elementary level would say that it was their least favorite subject. I would respond with a quip: "How then will you teach mathematics effectively?" Needless to say, I heard many interesting responses! Teachers need to determine their primary role and prepare earnestly for that role.

As a teacher or teacher-to-be, one must be a lifelong learner and a student of the subject matter to be taught. One must stay current in the field and continue to grow. As well, one must know how various subject matter should be learned. In the state of Pennsylvania, in which I reside and teach, teachers must study the structure of the subjects they will teach so that the approach and methods used for learning a particular subject will fit its nature and how it should be learned—a reflection of the past and Jerome Bruner, now again a focus of the twenty-first century.

Can you articulate the differences in ways of knowing and understanding inherent in science, history, literature and the language arts, music, the visual arts, biblical studies, social studies, and mathematics? For example: Which of the following subjects are more alike in how they are taught and learned, mathematics and the language arts or mathematics and science? Why? I often ask my classes this question. While it does take some thought, the immediate answer is usually that math and science are more alike, because math is used to measure, quantify, and communicate findings in science and these subjects are often coupled together. However, as to structure that determines how the subjects should be learned and thus taught, the language arts and mathematics are more alike. Both are very abstract and use symbols to communicate: human thoughts and feelings in language arts, and number and spatial relationships and patterns in mathematics. On the other hand, science is the most concrete of all subjects. A teacher will use hands-on, minds-on activities from kindergarten through a PhD program in science. Hands-on materials in mathematics, however, are designed to break down the abstraction until the student develops the concept, after which symbols must be used if the student is to experience continued success in mathematics.

Know the students and how they learn best:

Referring to the section of your developing philosophy on human learning, write at least one summary statement that connects human nature and learning to the role of the teacher. All sections of one's philosophy should be integrated together to form a coherent whole in spite of the fact that in this book we are examining the elements of education under separate headings. The document should become a unified whole.

Know how to bring together an understanding of the student learner and the subject matter to be learned:

Part of this topic has already been addressed under the nature of the learner and the implications for lesson planning. More will be addressed under the nature and purpose of the curriculum.

To Be in Charge

· Be a role model

Be in charge

If it is true that to teach is the primary role of the teacher, then to be in charge is secondary. However, this role is very much related to the promotion of learning. What do you think it means to **be in charge**? *teachers should be afraid*

Activity | Examining Authority

One category that could be created from the biblical passages earlier in this chapter is the role of "authority." The apostle Paul was not ashamed of his authority and he reveals why. In our educational culture today, teachers are often afraid to say that they are the authority in the classroom. Why do you think this is so?

Years ago, psychoanalytic theorist Sigmund Freud promoted the idea that needing to submit to an authority is a sign of psychological weakness and inferiority. The "need" for an authority and the resultant submission was deemed unhealthy. Submission to an authority was considered a personality "crutch." Freud's idea about authority fueled some of the rhetoric of the feminist movement of the 1970s. Some feminists spoke critically about the concept of mutual submission to other humans, submission of wives to husbands in a marriage relationship, and submission of humans to God. The concept of authority was therefore relegated to a shelf, labeled as an archaic concept no longer needed in the modern world. Teacher as authority became passé. Further complicating the matter was the fact that the cultural character of authority had remained a projection of the factory boss, a model that dominated even Christian circles. In addition, the outgrowth of the conclusions of the "active self" psychologists, the adoption of an atheistic form of Existentialism, and the promotion of the idea that the self is god by New Age thinkers led to the cultural thinking that no person needs an authority. Each person is autonomous and self-governing.

When reading the passage in 2 Corinthians 10:8 affirming the authority of a leader, a Christian who is influenced by the culture may be timid or unwilling to say that one of the roles of the teacher is the role of an authority. Most of my graduate students agree. In fact, even I use the term "in charge" in order not to hinder communication with teachers who have been strongly influenced by the cultural views of "authority," until I have a chance to explain the concept as I understand it. However, knowing my subject and being in charge (and thus taking responsibility for learning and the learning environment) is the task of one who is an authority in the classroom. Whether or not we wish to be in charge, we are. The government considers teachers to be the legal authority in the classroom, so we are held responsible legally for our students. It is the law of the land, at least in the United States. This is one reason why teachers must carry liability insurance.

The issue is not whether or not we are an authority in the classroom; rather, the issue concerns how we view the source of our authority, how we understand the kind of authority we have, how we view the character of authority, and what we see as the purpose of authority. Let us examine briefly the concept of authority to help clarify our thinking.

What characteristics of biblical authority must inform our role? Some questions to ponder:

- What is the **source** of authority?

- What **kind** of authority do teachers have (moral or legal)?

- What should be the **character** of one in authority?

- What is the **purpose** of authority?

Activity	The Source and Purpose of Authority

Look at the Scripture passage in 2 Corinthians 10:8 to answer some of these questions.

For even if I boast somewhat freely about the authority the Lord gave us for building you up rather than pulling you down, I will not be ashamed of it.

Based on this verse, from what source does the authority come? Is the primary source the teacher, the administration, the state, or something or someone else?

For what purpose is authority given?

To Consider

Have you ever told a class of students that you are "the BOSS"? Have you ever thought that the authority to be in charge was sourced in you as a person? Have you ever demanded respect, thinking, "You must respect me; I am the authority in this classroom." Where did you get these ideas? Are they not residual mindsets from the industrial factory model description of "bosses" rather than a biblical view? Who alone in all the universe has the right to be labeled "boss" (sovereign) because the authority is sourced in Himself? Consider the passage above, "the authority the Lord gave us . . ." It is a delegated authority. Jesus said to his disciples, "All authority in heaven and on earth has been given to me" (Matthew 28:18), then He told them to go into all the world and preach the gospel. All authority in the universe (other than God's) is delegated authority. It is sourced in God Himself. There is no place for a teacher to "lord it over" her charges:

> Be shepherds of God's flock that is under your care, serving as overseers—not because you must, but because you are willing, as God wants you to be; not greedy for money, but eager to serve; not lording it over those entrusted to you, but being examples to the flock.
>
> —1 Peter 5:2–3

Analysis

First, according to Scripture, authority is delegated from the Lord (2 Corinthians 10:8). But it is also delegated by the administrator in your school, the school board, the state, and any other body over you. From where do these people and institutions get their authority? Ultimately, all authority is from God, and He delegates that role to others. Since the authority does not reside in you, it might be counterproductive to refer to yourself as "the boss." In charge, yes! Boss, no!

What Kind of Authority Is Delegated?

In the book *The Emperor's New Clothes: The Naked Truth About the New Psychology* (1985), William K. Kilpatrick addresses the kind of authority teachers and parents may have.

> If we are all fellow citizens, what right do you have to tell me what to do? That is the way the child or adolescent will reason. They have learned that government (in our country) is by consent. Traditional modes of authority divorced from any concept of the sacred or natural order will appear as arbitrary impositions of will. The result? Even the most lenient schools and families will be viewed as aggressive (p. 70).

Comment: according to Kilpatrick, legal authority without moral authority will seem to be imposing a person's will (teacher) on a student and will lead to aggressive behavior. He goes on to say,

> Adults will experience increased resentment toward children. If children are simply fellow citizens rather than a sacred trust, it is difficult to see why one should sacrifice for them. Parents and teachers will reason that they owe nothing but the minimum legal requirements—they are mere custodians (p. 70).

Is the teacher a legal custodian? Moral authority? Or what?

What Is Moral Authority?

Moral authority is a philosophical concept that should serve as a basis for, but is not in itself a rule of written law. The moral authority and legitimacy of law can be based on metaphysics or religion, on nature, on some aspect of society, or on the individual. It may be referred to as a "higher law", involving right reason, which calls a person to the performance of their duties and restrains them from doing wrong.

Constitutional democracy combines qualitative, substantive, "higher law" concepts of justice and universal equality derived primarily from classical civilization and Judeo-Christian religion with quantitative, procedural concepts of justice and equality derived primarily from the communitarian ethic of common law, republican traditions, and social contract theory.

—U.S. Legal Definitions

Activity Reflect

What do you think? What kind of authority do teachers have? Read the definition of moral authority above; think about the definition in light of a Christian view of leadership, and determine whether or not a teacher's role is one of moral authority and why.

Write your thoughts here:

Can you find any references in Scripture (the Judeo-Christian religion referred to in the definition above) to help you draw your conclusion? Would you agree that moral authority goes well beyond legal authority to include special care for those under your charge? Would you agree that the delegated authority a leader has in addition to legal authority is a moral authority, a higher law, that seeks to promote human flourishing?

Summarize your thinking here:

Sociologist Richard Arum, addressing the problems of discipline in America public schools, adds his research to the investigation of moral and legal authority. He claims that the loss of moral authority in the schools began in the 1960s and '70s with the focus on autonomous individual rights. He believes that understanding the erosion of moral authority in school discipline "requires one to consider how the expansion of individual rights has come into conflict with the schools' prerogative to control student behavior" (Arum 2003, pp. 5–6). He concludes that U.S. court litigation (he called it adversarial legalism) and a sense of student entitlement have led to the problems in classroom discipline we have been experiencing in recent years. Legal authority has remained, but moral authority has been lost.

Cultural issues related to the role of the teacher as one in charge (in authority) must be examined in light of what it means to exercise authority as delegated by God and under His authority, rather than as arbitrary personal power. In the book of Jeremiah, the prophet writes, "A horrible and shocking thing has happened in the land: the prophets prophesy lies, the priests **rule by their own authority**" (5:30–31a). The outcome was disastrous for the people of Israel.

The Christian has a standard and a source of authority to help him to see both legal and moral issues more clearly. Understanding a biblical view will help the teacher focus on governance in the classroom, socialization practices, the identifying of right and wrong behaviors, the observing of legal issues or school law, and discipline from God's perspective. His pattern declares that discipline should be exercised out of love and for the profit of the human, "that we may share in his holiness" (His character) and experience "a harvest of righteousness and peace" (Hebrews 12:5–11). This would be a nice result of good biblical discipline—peace in the classroom. The purpose for discipline is for the profit—or good—or growth of the student, not control. A nonchaotic classroom (control, if you will) is a by-product of good discipline, rather than the goal. I believe that this biblical view will lead to the goal of human flourishing in the classroom.

According to the U.S. Legal definition, "Moral authority is based on metaphysics, religion, or nature." In what ways do you think that biblical Christianity upholds the moral authority of an educator (leader or teacher)?

Activity | Research

Find several verses that might help you to defend and describe the moral responsibility teachers might have as teachers of children. For example: Mark 9:36–37.

From the list of verses in the beginning of this chapter, determine the main idea related to a leader's responsibility. Here are two passages from that list:

1 Thessalonians 2:7–8

But we were gentle among you, like a mother caring for her little children. We loved you . . . we were delighted to share . . . our lives.

1 Thessalonians 2:11–12

For you know that we dealt with each of you as a father deals with his own children, encouraging, comforting and urging you to live lives worthy of God, who calls you into his kingdom and glory.

From a Christian perspective, it appears that the educator/leader has moral authority (delegated by God) and, under the governance of the state or country (also delegated by God), has legal authority as well. Moral authority requires the development and sharing of characteristics that are like those of the ideal mother or ideal father. The writer of 1 Thessalonians also called the ones to whom he wrote "brothers." A learning community that is based upon biblical ideas will be a loving, caring, nurturing, encouraging community, much like the ideal family might be.

The Purpose of Authority

Early in my career as an educator, I served as assistant dean of women at a small college where I was also teaching part-time. While serving there, the assistant dean of men and I decided to do some group counseling of students who were newlyweds. As we sat around the table of mostly new husbands (whose wives were working their husbands through college), we discussed issues that might help them grow as spouses, even while under the pressure of student life in a college setting. During one discussion, one man, married for just six months, said, "I require my wife to ask permission before she uses the telephone." Now, I was a teacher, not really a counselor; so instead of asking him to tell me more about his feelings, or what he was thinking, I blurted out, "What? Why do you do that?" His reply was worse, in my view, than his original statement: "I want her to know who is boss." I was sure that she would indeed know very soon and there might even be a divorce in the near future. I was far more certain, however, that he did not have a clue about the purpose for biblical authority, nor did he understand the biblical character of authority. I suspect that some Christians who are also teachers have distorted views of authority absorbed from culture and need some correction from the Word of God.

Activity	The Purpose of Authority

What is the purpose of authority? Underline the key part of this passage that refers to purpose.

For even if I boast somewhat freely about the authority the Lord gave us for building you up rather than pulling you down, I will not be ashamed of it. —2 Corinthians 10:8

The purpose of the apostle Paul's authority used to discipline a man in the church at Corinth was not for tearing down, but building up, edifying. The **character of authority** as reviewed in these passages is servanthood not kingship!

Character of Authority

I have spoken to hundreds, maybe thousands of teachers on this topic and have had several respond to me that if they were servants to their kids, the kids would walk all over them like a doormat. Perhaps you are thinking along the same lines. One response might be to point to Jesus Christ, who came to earth to serve rather than to be served and yet is the sovereign God of the universe. Some educational theorists, such as A. S. Neill, founder of the Summerhill School in the U.K., actually wrote that love and authority are antithetical. A person (whether a parent or teacher) cannot show both. And yet we see perfect love in Jesus, a servant who humbled himself and became a man, and still remained the authority, very God. Just take a look at John 13, where Jesus is manifesting a servant's heart and actions as He washes the feet of His disciples. Afterward He said, "You call me 'Teacher' and 'Lord,' and rightly so, for that is what I am" (authority). However, the passage begins, "Having loved his own who were in the world ..." (John 13:1) and ends with a command to serve each other (John 13:17). Loving servant, yes! Authority and Lord, yes! Both. A. S. Neill was wrong.

The temptation of the disciples, you may remember, was to want to be first, and yet Jesus rebuked them and taught them in Mark 10:42–45:

> You know that those who are regarded as rulers of the Gentiles lord it over them, and their high officials exercise authority over them. Not so with you. Instead, whoever wants to become great among you must be your servant, and whoever wants to be first must be slave of all. For even the Son of Man did not come to be served, but to serve, and to give his life as a ransom for many.

Perhaps that instruction led Peter to write in 1 Peter 5:2–3:

> Be shepherds of God's flock that is under your care, serving as overseers—not because you must, but because you are willing, as God wants you to be; not greedy for money, but eager to serve; not lording it over those entrusted to you, but being examples to the flock.

And led Paul to write in 1 Thessalonians 2:7–12:

> We were gentle among you, like a mother caring for her children. We loved you so much.... We dealt with each of you as a father deals with his own children, encouraging, comforting and urging you to live lives worthy of God.

Roles of teacher
to teach = know material / know how to teach
to serve
be in charge
be a role model

Conclusion

The role of the teacher is a delegated role to be in charge, not to lord it over as boss, but to be a servant-leader. There are legal and moral responsibilities. The teacher disciplines and instructs to edify, nurture, encourage, and correct—not to destroy, demean, or control, but to promote the good of the child. The student is a sacred trust.

There is a biblical mandate to love our students. I love the way writers Long and Frye address the call to love children and youth in the teaching profession in their book, *Making It Till Friday*:

> We regard love as *an attitude that expresses itself in a helping action.* On the other hand, *liking is an attitude that expresses itself in feelings of attraction to or fondness for others.* It would be nice to feel attracted to or fond of everyone, because helping them would then be easier. But is it really possible to be attracted to everyone at all times? Probably not. Furthermore pretending that one can like every student equally could eventually lead to disillusionment when that standard cannot be met. Teachers, however, *can take actions in the best interests of students*—regardless of how cantankerous or unlikable a student may be at a given moment. To us, that is love. As a matter of fact, philosopher-scholar C. S. Lewis (1952) says that *loving your enemies is easier when you recognize that you do not have to be fond of them.* (1985, pp. 15–16)

Activity	Write

Try to write a good paragraph on the role of the teacher as one in charge but there to serve.

The Teacher as a Role Model

Would you have signed this contract?

> Your pay will be $5.00 a month, providing you meet these conditions:
> 1. Don't get married and don't keep company with men.
> 2. Don't be away from home between the hours of 8 P.M. and 6 A.M.
> 3. Don't loiter in ice cream parlors.
> 4. Don't smoke cigarettes; don't drink beer, wine, or whiskey.
> 5. Don't leave town without permission.
> 6. Don't ride in a carriage or automobile with any man except your father or brother.
> 7. Don't dress in bright colors, dye your hair, or use face powder, mascara, or lipstick.
>
> *Original source unknown…thought to be Idaho teacher's contract, dated 1923.*

Now perhaps this is going too far.

When I was a student in elementary school many years ago, teachers were influenced by the educational thinking of the day and the concept of modeling the upstanding citizen. The upstanding citizen was a respected reflection of the society in which we lived and was thought to be the best of the best. Teachers were not allowed to smoke in public, drink in public, nor to be seen at "houses of ill repute." Even actors and actresses who played the role of teachers on TV were not to be seen doing things that might influence school children in the wrong way. How times have changed! In fact, if indeed the teacher is the upstanding citizen and should be a role model to students, as educators half a century ago suggested, then the target for what we are to model changes from decade to decade and maybe year to year. Try to describe an upstanding citizen (in the 1950s, for example), and then compare that with today's "upstanding citizen." Try to compare the 1980s or even the 1990s with today.

How do we as Christian teachers determine after whom or what we pattern our modeling? Do we follow the moving target of the culture, or do we have an unchanging, immovable target?

Activity | Modeling Christ

The apostle Paul wrote to his readers to be followers "of me as I am a follower of Christ."

Perhaps we can start there. What does it mean to model Christ? That is, what does it look like and sound like?

Take a brief minute and write your thoughts here:

Role Modeling and the Aim of Education

Glorifying God by manifesting what He is like on earth is a primary aim of life for the Christian. Since the aim of education is connected to the aim of life, the aim of education that follows might be that the student will develop fully as an image-bearer and flourish as God intended, all to His glory. What does that look like? What are the characteristics that humans should reflect and teachers should model?

For years, I wondered what it looked like to reflect the glory of the Lord. Then one day while reading the Bible and studying for a retreat ministry, I read a passage in Exodus in which Moses was asked by God to be the servant-leader of the Israelites as they moved on toward the Promised Land. Moses was not all that excited about leading these stubborn people, so he had a lot of questions to ask the Lord: "Who will go with me? What else will distinguish me and your people from all the other people on the face of the earth?" The Lord replied that His Presence would go with Moses. Then Moses said, "Show me your glory." The Lord said that He would and he did. Now, have you ever wondered how to manifest the glory of the Lord in your life? Here is what the Lord showed Moses as He demonstrated before him His glory.

> And he passed in front of Moses, proclaiming, 'The LORD, the LORD, the compassionate and gracious God, slow to anger, abounding in love and faithfulness, maintaining love to thousands, and forgiving wickedness, rebellion and sin. —Exodus 34:6–7a

As I read the story and the description of the Lord's glory (in this case, His presence), I had an aha! moment: You mean the glory of the Lord is not some ethereal, out-of-this-world thing, like some Star Wars-type spooky sound track? It is rather very straightforward: The glory of the Lord is, in part, His presence and His character. God's character is manifested in who He is as . . .

The compassionate, the gracious God;

Slow to anger, abounding in love,

Faithful, and forgiving.

I had also been studying the book of Colossians for the retreat and found the following: "Christ in you, the hope of glory" (Colossians 1:27). And then, in Colossians 3:12–14:

Therefore as God's chosen people, holy and dearly loved, clothe yourselves with compassion, kindness, humility, gentleness and patience. Bear with each other and forgive.... And over all these virtues put on love.

Compare the two sets of descriptions, the one that declares the glory of God in Exodus and the one that declares the characteristics that manifest Christ-likeness in Colossians.

The glory of the Lord (Exodus 34:6, 7)	Christ in you, the hope of glory (Colossians 3:12–14)
And he passed in front of Moses, proclaiming, 'The LORD, the LORD, the compassionate and gracious God, slow to anger, abounding in love, and faithfulness, maintaining love to thousands, and forgiving wickedness, rebellion and sin...'	Therefore as God's chosen people. Holy and dearly loved. Clothe yourselves with compassion, kindness, humility, gentleness, and patience. Bear with one another and forgive. Over all these virtues, put on love.

Read also 2 Corinthians 3:18. "And we, who with unveiled faces all reflect the Lord's glory, are being transformed into his likeness with ever-increasing glory, which comes from the Lord."

For me, the problem was solved. The nonmoving target that answers the question who or what I model as a teacher/leader is simply the character of God, manifested in His glory and fleshed out in His son the Lord Jesus Christ. That also helped to answer the question I had about how to glorify God in my life. My life is to manifest Christ's characteristics, visible as He walked the earth and served as a teacher to the disciples. We model Christ. No wonder the Apostle Paul said, "Follow my example, as *I follow the example of Christ*" (1 Corinthians 11:1). How dynamic our classrooms would be if we were modeling compassion, forgiveness, faithfulness, gentleness, patience, and love. I want to be like that!

To summarize, the role of the teacher is:

- **To teach**, knowing the students and the subject matter and bringing the two together in effective learning,

- **To serve** as a caring shepherd,

- **To be in charge** over, and responsible for, the care of the students and the learning environment for edification not destruction and control, and

- **To be a role model**—of Christ, manifesting the glory of the Lord in our lives.

I love the poem "Christ in You," by Beatrice Cleland. It is a poem that highlights the concept of modeling in attitude and actions, in little things (many of which a teacher will experience in a classroom). But it also points out the person we model and the end result of the role model.

Christ in You by Beatrice Clelland

Not merely by the words you say

Nor in your deeds confessed

But in the most unconscious way is Christ expressed.

Is it a beatific smile upon your face

A holy light upon your brow

Oh yes, I felt his presence while you laughed just now.

For me t'was not the truth you taught

So clear to you, to me still dim

But when you came to me you brought a sense of him.

And from your eyes he beckons me

And from your heart his love is shed

Until I lose sight of you and see the Christ instead.

(as cited in Woychuk, N.A., 1962)

Engage mind

access brain

11 | **The Nature of the Curriculum**

The final section of an educational philosophy, as outlined in this book, is about the curriculum. I find that describing the nature of the curriculum is not as straightforward as one might think. Even seasoned teachers have a difficult time. Many teachers think that the curriculum is a spiral-bound teacher's edition of a text or a guide for subject matter and delivery handed to them a month before they begin the school year. The purpose of the curriculum is often not addressed at all. The purpose must be informed by the aim of education in general (section one of this book). If the aim of education has not been identified, it is difficult to establish an overarching purpose for the curriculum. We will address both the purpose and the nature of the curriculum, beginning with its nature.

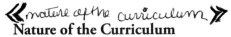

Nature of the Curriculum

To begin the exploration of the nature of the curriculum, I like to ask the following question of my students, both undergraduates and teachers returning for graduate education: "How many of you have ever taken a curriculum course?" Interestingly, many who have taken multiple pedagogy courses without the word *curriculum* in the title are very unsure. All those who have taken a course with the word curriculum in it answer in the affirmative. Students are then asked to describe the term *curriculum* in pairs or threes, using a concept map. Students draw an egg on a piece of paper and connect as many words as come to mind related to the curriculum. Try to do that now by describing the term *curriculum* using the oval on the following page and as many descriptors as come to your mind.

engage mind and
curriculum includes
O : lesson plan

Try your hand at creating a concept map or list descriptors.

Elements of the curriculum are . . .

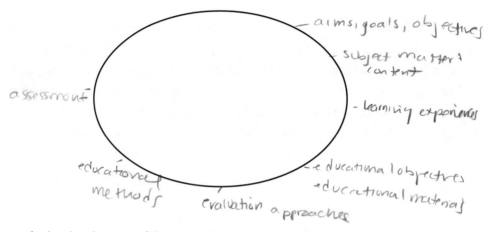

- aims, goals, objectives
- subject matter/content
- learning experiences
- educational objectives
- educational material

assessment

educational methods

evaluation approaches

If you prefer, list the elements of the curriculum:

Finish the sentence: The curriculum may be described as...

This activity should lead to the dissolution of the idea that the curriculum is simply the text, the guide, the standards, or the materials that a teacher is handed by the administration to use for a particular course or for the year. These, of course, are important. They are the curricular materials. They do not, however, represent the whole of the curriculum.

Categorize the elements of the curriculum you have listed or included in your concept map. A typical set of categories may include: plans, delivery, and the planned environment for learning. Typical sub-elements include: scope and sequence (what will be addressed and in what order), materials that will be used, goals and standards to target, the methods to be used to carry out the plan, and the planned optimal environment or learning community.

Activity | Free Write

In the chart on the next page, free write all that you believe about these three categories: plans, delivery, and environment. These elements of the curriculum serve as a framework to help you address the nature of the curriculum.

If you are completing this book with other students, share your thinking and determine why you believe what you do about each area. Describe the focus of the curriculum for traditional and progressive philosophies as you understand them to be, and compare these ideas to your own thinking.

Plans What will yours include?	
Delivery How will you carry out the plan?	
Environment What kind of learning community atmosphere do you intend to create?	

The Nature of the Curriculum Is Related to How Humans Learn

As you work through the process of examining, clarifying, and writing your beliefs, it will become apparent that the parts of your educational philosophy are interrelated. The strong connection between the curriculum, the nature of the student and learning (chapters 5–9), and the role of the teacher will be evident as you think and write about the nature of the curriculum. Your final philosophy of education document should be an internally consistent set of beliefs that coheres in such a way that it makes sense as a unified whole. To highlight this process, answer the following questions:

1. What will I do differently in my curricular plans and delivery if I believe that the student is an active participant in his own learning with an interactive actional nature, rather than either a passive receiver of information or an autonomously active creator of his own personal knowledge or reality?

2. What will I do differently in my plans and delivery if I understand my students' developmental limits and potentials, both grade level and individual? What will I consider and how will that affect the curriculum and my behaviors as a teacher?

3. How will I respond to students if I believe that humans are created in the image of God? What value will I place on each life? How will my behaviors reflect my beliefs as I work with the poorest child, the most gifted, the learning disabled, the ELL (English Language Learner), the worst behaved, or the brightest and the best academically? (The answer will be reflected in your plan for an effective learning community.)

Decide what will impact your understanding of the nature of the curriculum by using what you have already processed and written about as you worked through the chapters on the nature of the student and learning and the role of the teacher.

In chapter 5 we examined traditional and progressive views of education. How would those who hold to one of these philosophies describe the curriculum? Below is a chart of possible general beliefs held by each.

- Keeps teacher in target
  It is not neutral

what a curriculum includes:

Category	Traditional	Progressive
Plans (Lesson Plan)	Facts, skills, content, quiz	Process, activities, experiences
Delivery	Dispense information, tell, put in	Student activities, draw out
Environment	Rigid, stern, business-like	Permissive, relaxed, free
Labels	**Subject-centered**	**Student-centered**

Notice the labels for the curriculum in the chart above: "student-centered" and "subject-centered." The nature of the curriculum has often been labeled in curriculum theory and design books as "student-centered," "subject-centered," "society (citizen)-centered," or "teacher-centered."

Activity   Matching

Match the labels that represent the nature of the curriculum for the traditional and progressive philosophies of education listed as a–d below. (See Appendix One for brief descriptions of the modern philosophies of education.)

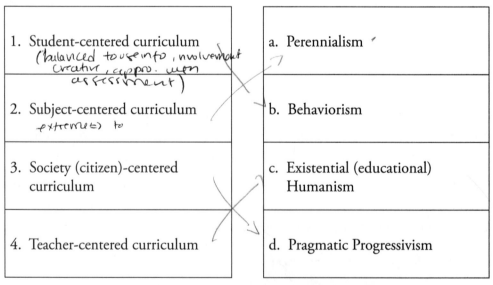

1. Student-centered curriculum
   (balanced to use info, involvement creative, appro. uep assessment)

2. Subject-centered curriculum
   extremes) to

3. Society (citizen)-centered curriculum

4. Teacher-centered curriculum

a. Perennialism

b. Behaviorism

c. Existential (educational) Humanism

d. Pragmatic Progressivism

Answers: 1c; 2a; 3d; 4b. (a and b are traditional and c and d are progressive views)

Interactive = / passive nature

interaction actional nature describes it best

Perennialism favors the subject matter of the classics, Behaviorism focuses on the role of the teacher as a reinforcer to promote learning behaviors, Educational Humanism champions a child-centered focus along with the choosing agent and decision-maker emphases of Existentialism, and Progressivism focuses on what works (Pragmatism) to produce good citizens for a democracy.

Decide which label you would use for the general nature of the curriculum: Subject-centered? Standards-centered? Student-centered? Teacher-centered? Citizen-centered? Or something else? Why? The study of human learning may help you understand the underlying beliefs and central focus of the curriculum. Have you determined the relative importance of content and process/experience? Review your definition of education from chapter 3 and how you came to your conclusion regarding the "kind" of learning you wish to promote. These elements of your philosophy might help you select a label for the focus of the curriculum.

An Alternate View

As a young teacher, I struggled with the question related to the general nature of the curriculum. I believed that the student was the central figure in education, but I also saw a huge role for the teacher and content. I realized that the student was in school to learn something. As a middle school teacher, I felt there was no need to label the focus of the curriculum; I knew what I believed. However, when I started teaching a philosophy of education course, there was an inner pressure to find a label with which I was personally comfortable. The label I landed on was simply "learning-centered."

For many years, the wars between "subject-centered" and "student-" or "child-entered" curricula had been waged on the pages of journals such as *Educational Leadership* and in yearbooks of the Association of Supervision and Curriculum Development (ASCD). Finally, several years ago, after presenting the pendulum swings between subject- and student-centered curricula for years, prestigious educational organizations came out with the label "learner-centered," connoting that a student is **learning** something. Principles were developed by an APA Work Group of the Board of Educational Affairs (1997).

In addition to my recommended label, "learning-centered," I also use a label that is now quite popular among educators and curriculum designers: "learner-centered curriculum." These descriptors move the focus from teaching or from

children need to outside of inside info to learn

student development alone to the student *coming to know* something as the learning event is orchestrated by a knowledgeable teacher. Learning connotes change in thinking and acting. You decide on your own label. Be able to defend your choice.

The curriculum should promote student learning, and therefore the teacher must take into account how humans learn as a primary consideration. If you go back and review the beliefs committed to and addressed in previous sections of this text, you might come up with something like the following to describe the nature of the curriculum:

The primary components of the curriculum are:

Learning Plans (overall approach to teaching or teaching model):

Plans for promoting student learning that focus on content that is student-processed and understood for retrieval and use in problem solving, decision making, and growing as a learner ˌHook, Objective,

Learning Activities (delivery methods):

Impressive and expressive methods to carry out a cognitive interactive learning plan

Learning Community (planned classroom environment):

Planned environment that promotes student learning and human flourishing in a caring community

Nature of the Content or Subject Matter of the Curriculum

While the nature of the student and learning is addressed thoroughly in most schools of education today, a second question related to the curriculum is not. That question concerns the content of learning: "What is the nature of the 'what' that students learn?"

When educators discuss the curriculum, they must, on the one hand, discuss the nature of the human learner, and on the other hand, discuss the nature of knowledge and knowing. All educational philosophers do this and so must we.

The second issue is more difficult than the first, simply because there is currently more diverse thinking related to questions about the nature of the curricular content than about the nature of the learner. Those informed by a Christian worldview will generally find themselves more opposed to the current-day, avant-garde views of the nature of knowledge than to current-day views on the nature of the learner. Writing a philosophy of education is an activity that demands the integration of knowledge found in our discipline of education with a biblical worldview. Where will that take us as we grapple with the "what" that students learn?

If we know what we believe, we can be exposed to and study any current or past thinking of others, assimilating what fits with our worldview and rejecting that which contradicts our worldview. Knowing what we believe enables a more open-minded approach that allows us to investigate an issue and work through it. Exercise in biblical integration using a worldview approach requires critical thinking skills, that is, "*evaluating and judging based upon some standard*"; or "*considering new ideas or information in light of one's previous beliefs*"; or "*examination of an idea or product in light of some norm or standard.*"

One of the most accepted definitions of critical thinking was provided many years ago by William Sumner (1911): "[Critical thinking is] the examination and test of propositions of any kind which are offered for acceptance, in order to find out whether they correspond to reality or not" (p. 632). *Discern good and bad*

In the case of an informed Christian philosophy, the standards are biblical answers to life's biggest questions or the major questions addressed in any worldview.

The question about the "what" we learn or the content in the curriculum was addressed many years ago by evolutionary philosopher and sociologist Herbert Spencer (1820–1903). In the mid-1800s, he asked the question this way: "What knowledge is of most worth?" He wrote:

> Before there can be a rational *curriculum*, we must settle which things it most concerns us
> to know… We must determine the relative values of knowledges (Spencer 1864, p. 29).

As a social scientist and naturalist, Spencer's conclusion was that science is the most important knowledge to know and, in fact, it should replace the classical languages, which in his view were of little practical use. Not all agreed.

— plans
— Delivery
— environment

Different philosophical perspectives emphasize different subject matter as their integrating core knowledge, "the knowledge most worth knowing." This core provides meaning for the curriculum as a whole and fortifies the understood purpose for the curriculum. Spencer chose science. Match the following: Which modern philosophy of education would choose each focus or integrating core of the curriculum? (See Appendix One for brief descriptions of the modern philosophies of education a–e.)

The focus or integrating core of the curriculum should be...	Modern philosophies of education
1. Math and science	a. Essentialism
2. Classics and the Great Books	b. Perennialism
3. Self-esteem, choosing and decision-making	c. Behaviorism
4. Foundational knowledge and basic skills	d. Progressivism
5. Vocational, technological, useful skills and knowledge	e. Educational Humanism

Answers: 1c; 2b; 3e; 4a; 5d

The point of the above matching activity is to demonstrate that differing educational perspectives lead to the selection of different curricular integrating cores. Each view selects the knowledge "most worth knowing" as its integrating content or set of ideas. This does not mean that other knowledge areas or disciplines are unimportant. For example, a private school or magnet or charter school may select the fine arts, or the natural sciences, or mathematics, or vocational preparation, or the classics as the integrating core around which other subject areas are organized. Theoretically, this approach gives meaning and motivation to the learners. All other subjects are related in some way to the integrating core. An educational philosophy informed by a Christian worldview will also select an integrating core. How would you answer the questions, "*What knowledge is most worth knowing, and why?*" The consideration of the integrating core will be addressed again in this chapter.

The "What" Our Students Learn

What is the source and validity of knowledge? Is it outside the knower or inside the knower? Is it objective or subjective?

We have already addressed the two historically competing views on the nature of the human in the learning event (active and passive), as well as the more recent third view (interactive). There have also been two historic views related to the nature of knowledge and knowing. These are: (1) the human is a passive receiver of objective truth that is taken in photographically, and (2) the human is an active creator of his own personal truth. And the war goes on! The worldview issue addressed here is, *What is the nature of knowledge and human knowing?* Both issues (knowledge and knowing) must be examined as they relate to learning and therefore addressed in an instructional philosophy.

Various philosophical positions espouse different views on this issue. Herbert Spencer would have taken the first view: objective (scientific) truth is the most vital knowledge for learning. The second view is taken by William Doll, author of *A Post-modern Perspective on Curriculum* (1993), who compared content-centered (traditional/scientific) and student-centered (progressive/humanistic) curricula. He reported that the dominance of scientific, technical rationality has trivialized education. It has reduced the curriculum to controlled measurable fragments. He went on to declare:

> Educationally, we need to be trained in the art of creating and choosing, not just in ordering and following. Much of our curriculum to date has trained us to be passive receivers of preordained 'truths' not active creators of knowledge* (p. 8).

Activity | Evaluate

Evaluate Doll's quote above in light of the nature of the student and learning and the nature of knowledge and knowing. Which of these two positions about knowledge is correct: active creator of knowledge or passive receiver of preordained 'truths'? Or is there a third viewpoint? Defend your position. (Doll, in the previous quote, would take the autonomously active human side of the pendulum and lean toward a postmodern view of knowledge that declares that the human is a creator of reality.)

---

*For a full-blown study of postmodern curricular theory, see *Curriculum Development in the Postmodern Era (2nd Ed.)* by Patrick Slattery (2006).

For thought: In *The Death of Truth*, Dennis McCallum writes:

Now, in the late twentieth century, we are in the middle of a revolution that will likely dwarf Darwinism in its impact on every aspect of thought and culture: the revolution is postmodernism, and the danger it holds in its most serious form is that truth, meaning, and objective reality do not exist, and that all religious beliefs and moral codes are subjective (1996, p. 12).

One of the central tenets of the postmodern era we live in is that there is no such thing as objective truth. In fact, the new trend in postmodern thought is to embrace, affirm, and live with philosophical, theological, and even scientific chaos. Truth may be true for one person and false for another. Truth has become a function of personal preference or personal construction, rather than correspondence to an objective reality or what is the case (McCallum). Those who express their ideas about objectivity and subjectivity—who are concerned with **how** humans learn *and* **what** they learn—usually fall somewhere on a continuum between the two.

Objective   **Subjective**

Cognitive interactive theorists also fall at various places on the objective/subjective continuum when they describe the nature of knowledge *and* knowing. Those who hold clearly to the belief that human learning involves inside and outside factors working together in the learning event (actional nature is "interactive") do not all agree on the nature and source of knowledge. Some hold that the human constructs *meanings* and *understandings*, while not essentially changing the thing known. They separate the known and the knower in their view of knowledge and knowing. Inside and outside factors are equally important in learning. Both exist in their own right. Objectivity in describing the nature of knowledge is retained.

Others do not separate the known and the knower and focus more heavily on inside factors. They do not affirm or deny a world of knowledge or truth outside the knower, but rather affirm that if there is reality separate from the knower, it cannot be known. They hold that humans *create their own personal knowledge*. This latter view is a far more subjective view of knowledge and knowing.

Activity An Example

Below is an illustration used to demonstrate, with understated simplicity, three different views of knowledge and knowing. With which one do you agree? The story concerns three baseball umpires discussing their craft of calling balls and strikes. Remember that in baseball, there is an **outside objective standard** for a strike: the width and length of home plate and the distance between the knees and the letters across the chest of the uniform of the player. The standard is in the rule book, but human umpires do the calling! Keep this in mind as you read the illustration.

Discussing the problems of their profession	Thinking
The first umpire said, "Some are balls, and some are strikes, and I call them as they are."	Strikes are objective in their own right, and I perceive them as a photograph! How could I be wrong?
The second said, "I see them coming, and some are balls, and some are strikes, but they aren't anything until I call them."	A strike is relative to my seeing and calling it! It is what it is to me. I create the strike or ball. I am never wrong.
The third said, "Some are balls, and some are strikes according to the standard, and I call them as I see them."	Strikes are determined by an objective standard, but I bring my sight and thought to the strike and call it! I try to get it right, but could be wrong.

Only one of the umpires would benefit from assessment (that is, a "boo," or whistle, finger snaps, or applause). Which one? Why?

What are three possible views of knowledge *and* knowing/learning that can be identified from the baseball illustration? (Each view's implications for the curriculum are in **bold** below.)

View One: Knowledge/reality exists outside the knowing mind and is totally objective and absolute. Don't confuse the issue by discussing something inside the knower. The focus is on the existence of the "stuff" known, rather than the knower.

This leads to a curricular focus on content and ignores inside factors of the student. Students are to take the teacher's notes and give them back exactly. All students should be able to learn equally well.

View Two: Knowledge/reality is constructed by the mind and is totally subjective and relative. The focus is on the knower as not separate from the known.

This leads to a focus on the student and process rather than on content. Students create their own personal knowledge. Hopefully, to those who hold this position, the knowledge is viable—that is, it is capable of working successfully in living.

View Three: Reality exists outside the knowing mind and is objective and absolute but is known rather subjectively because of the limits of the human mind and the limits of prior knowledge, vocabulary, etc. Knowledge exists in its own right, but there is someone coming to know what is there to be known.

This leads to a focus on content that is processed and understood in relation to the learner's prior knowledge, abilities, limits, vocabulary, and prior experience. Assessment is essential. Students can be right, partially right, or entirely wrong when measured by an outside standard. Assessment of understandings, skills, and meaning-getting is vital. *The focus is on the knower coming to know something.*

Activity | Consider Adler's Examples

Philosopher Mortimer Adler, introduced in chapter 7, took pride in writing that could be understood by the general population, and not just philosophers. He wanted all serious citizens to think about these issues. His illustrations are helpful. He states his own metaphor about the nature of what the student learns. Here again are his words.

> In general it can be said that knowing is not like eating. When we eat something, we take it into our bodies, digest it, assimilate it. It becomes part of us. It no longer remains what it was before it was eaten. But with one striking exception, our knowing something in no way affects or alters the thing known. We may take it into our minds in some way, but doing that leaves it exactly the same as it was before we knew it…

There is a sense in which knowing is like eating. The edible, before it is eaten, exists quite independently of the eater and is whatever it is regardless of how it is transformed by being eaten. So, too, the knowable exists quite independently of the knower and is whatever it is whether it is known or not, and however it is known.

The word most of us use to signify the independent character of the knowable is the word 'reality.' If there were no reality, nothing the existence and character of which is independent of the knowing mind, there would be nothing knowable. Reality is that which exists whether we think about it or not, and has the character that it has no matter how we think about it.

The reality that is knowable may or may not be physical. It may or may not consist solely of things perceptible to our senses. But whatever its character, its existence must be public, not private. It must be knowable by two or more persons. Nothing that is knowable by one person alone can have the status of knowledge (1985, pp. 88–89).

How does this quote relate to the baseball illustration?

Adler is presenting a contrast to the views of knowledge held by the pure naturalist/materialist who accepts as knowledge only those things "**solely** perceptible to our senses"; that view would certainly leave God out as "non-sense." It would also leave much of Adler's own field of philosophy outside the parameters of knowledge. The view of knowledge as "solely that which is perceptible to our senses," while based upon a presupposition or assumption of a particular worldview, resides clearly on the polar end of the continuum labeled "objective." To one who holds this view, knowledge exists in its own right, and it is learned as a photograph or dictation, if indeed it is learned. The assumption is that, to be valid, knowledge must be that which is verified by our senses alone.

Adler is also offering a contrasting view to the "philosophical mistake" (one of ten he is addressing in his book) made by postmodern thinkers who champion knowledge as solely personal and reality as that which is created by the mind. Adler's view seems to be the third view discussed in the illustration of the baseball umpires. Even if the third umpire got it wrong and called what was clearly a strike a ball (TV commentators and electronic devices will tell us), it does not change the fact that, according to the standard for balls and strikes, it was a strike. Of course, the error affects the game, little or much, and so too can faulty thinking!

If Adler is right, there is a real object (not just appearances) and a real subject— someone doing the knowing. Thus, we could say that according to Adler and others who have addressed coming to know under the epistemological labels of critical-realists or limited-realists, humans are in a position to know objective realities, yet know these objective realities with a measure of subjectivity because of our human limitations. Our understandings and meanings must therefore be "publicly" checked for accuracy, using the standards of knowledge available to humans: reason, experience, revelation, intuition, and authorities.

The baseball illustration helps educators begin to see that a perspective on knowledge will certainly filter into the curriculum. Even though it is beyond the scope of this book to develop an epistemology that fits with a biblical view of knowledge, introducing the topic may encourage some readers to take the time to do additional research and explore the topic in depth. It is a topic getting much attention today in our postmodern world and in the field of education as Radical Constructivism permeates curricular discussions.

While Adler was a twentieth century (1902—2001) philosopher, tackling the issue in the early 1980s, theologians have also addressed the same issue. For example, British theologian N. T. Wright offers the following:

> I propose a form of critical realism. This is a way of describing the process of 'knowing' that acknowledges the reality of the thing known, as something other than the knower (hence 'realism'), while also fully acknowledging that the only access we have to this reality lies along a path of appropriate dialogue or conversation between the knower and the thing known (hence 'critical'). This model allows fully for the actuality of knowledge beyond that of one's own sense-data (that which the 'objectivist' desires to safeguard), while also fully allowing for the involvement of the knower in the act of knowing (that upon which the 'subjectivist' will rightly insist) (1992, pp. 35–36, 47).

The Objective/Subjective Knowledge/Knowing Continuum

Objective   **Subjective**

How might the problem presented between the two ends of the objective and subjective continuum be solved? Is there a third view related to knowledge and knowing?

In *Love Your God With All Your Mind* (1997), J.P. Moreland briefly addresses the nature of knowledge and knowing, as he presents an overview of the mind as it relates to and interacts with the external world (outside factors). I appreciate Moreland's written work, especially when he is writing to the general public, including educators, and not just to theologians and philosophers. Below are some excerpts to whet your appetite for further research.

Moreland declares that indeed, "the body [senses] is the vehicle through which we interact with the world" (p. 65). But he goes on to discuss the body-soul (material-immaterial) unity of the human. Included in his description of the soul is the "mind":

> The mind is the faculty of the soul that contains thoughts and beliefs along with the relevant abilities to have such things. It is with my mind that I think, and my mind contains my beliefs (p. 72).

In describing the nature of knowledge and knowing, Moreland writes:

> The mind is the soul's primary vehicle for making contact with God... In thought, the **mind's structure conforms to the order of the object of thought** (p. 67, emphasis mine).

There is a **mind** (inner factor) and an **object** of thought (outer factor). Moreland declares that since God is a rational God and we are created in his image, the human ability to reason and think is a part of the image of God in mankind. And we can think and come to know what God has created, a knowable world. We were made to do so!

> The Old Testament proclaims that the same rational God who reveals Himself to the prophets

also created the world as an orderly, understandable cosmos. And the Old Testament assures us that this God made our minds to be apt for gaining knowledge and understanding so as to avoid foolish and ignorant beliefs. For those willing to pay the price of exercising their minds and studying diligently, there is knowledge and wisdom found in Scripture (Psalm 119); in the natural world and its operations (Isaiah 28:23–29); and in the accumulated insights embedded in the art, literature, and science of the different cultures of the world (Isaiah 19:11–13; Jeremiah 49:7; Daniel 2:12–13, 5:7) (pp. 66–67).

As wonderful as it is, the capacity to think, to reason, to come to know is in serious need of outside information about which to think and reason. Moreland cites information from the natural world, the Scriptures, and human insights from various cultures and artifacts. He claimed that the more we know, the more we can come to know and understand the world around us, and the more we can know God.

Transformation of the mind involves not only the inside facility to choose (will) and the desire to change (emotions), but also reasons to change that are often instructed by new information. The apostle Paul called for believers to be "transformed by the renewing of your mind" (Romans 12:2). Remember that our definition of learning includes "change in thinking and acting."

Content Knowledge Is Vital to the Thinking Mind

The content of a belief helps to determine how important the belief is for our character and behavior. **What** we believe matters—**the actual content** of what we believe about God, morality, politics, life after death, and so on will shape the contours of our lives and actions (Moreland 1997, p. 73, emphasis mine).

When Christian educators consider the curriculum and the question, "What is the nature and source of knowledge?" they must understand that something is there to be learned, an objective and knowable world in all its complexities and the God who created it, as well as *someone* doing the learning. Christian educators must also realize that coming to know is messy and involves a measure of subjectivity because of human limits in vocabulary, prior knowledge, processing capacities, and other complex cognitive and emotional factors. Teachers must be aware that standards of knowledge do matter, just like the baseball standard for a strike, yet cognitively interactive humans can misconstrue and misunderstand for a variety of reasons. Ongoing assessment is essential to learning and should be a form of feedback that lets students know whether or not they are "getting it"! Are they meeting the criteria or standard? Assessment is also feedback to the teacher that indicates whether or not the students are getting it—that is, whether they understand the information or can use the skill effectively.

Why might a person think that a view of knowledge and knowing that includes both inside factors and outside factors may fit best with a biblical view of knowledge and knowing? Does it? You decide.

<table>
<tr><td>**Activity**</td><td>**Discuss or Reflect**</td></tr>
</table>

Discuss or reflect on the above views of knowledge and knowing and the implications for education. Are there any hints in Scripture that affirm that outside information is vital, as well as the way it is processed by the learner? (Refer back to the discussion in chapter 3 about the kind of learning portrayed in Scripture.)

Importance of Understanding and Wisdom

"Knowledge is not the highest of intellectual goods. Of higher value is understanding, and beyond that, wisdom."

—Mortimer Adler, *Ten Philosophical Mistakes*, p. 107

Adler's statement is made as he champions philosophical thought that helps us "to understand everything else that we know" and, from understanding, gain "some measure of wisdom…."

It was in Colossians 1:9–10 that the apostle Paul *prayed* that the people in Colossae would *learn* a certain way (see chapter 3 of this book), "asking God to fill you with the *knowledge* of His will through spiritual *wisdom and understanding*," which then would impact all of life and growth and development.

Two Examples

To cognitive interactive theorists, understanding of new information is vital. So too is understanding vital in the learning events portrayed in Scripture. Take for example Acts 8, the story of the Ethiopian treasurer of Candace the queen, who believed in God, worshipped Him, read the book of Isaiah, and yet lacked complete understanding. God sent Philip to come along beside him and ask, "Do you understand what you are reading?" The Ethiopian answered, "How can I unless someone explains it to me? ... Tell me please, who is the prophet talking about, himself or some other?" (This was the content he was processing and trying to make sense out of.)

At the student's invitation, the teacher, Philip, began to explain that the passage in Isaiah 53 was talking about Jesus, and he shared with the Ethiopian the good news. After the explanation, the learner believed and asked to be identified with those who believed in Christ by being baptized. After this learning experience, he went on his way rejoicing. A transformed mind! What was the key to this change? *Understanding* of new information! He had already shown desire and the will to read and worship God, but he needed new additional information. The understanding was promoted by the teacher's use of the Scriptures at hand and the prompts of the student as he questioned and tried to understand. Outside factors (the truth of God's word, the teacher's explanation) and inside factors (the capacity to makes sense and to use prior knowledge, beliefs, and new information to clarify and learn) worked together in leading to a change in mind and behavior. This is learning!

Check also the parable of the sower, the seed, and the ground on which the seed fell in Matthew 13:18–23. The key is again "understanding." Notice the progression you find there. "When anyone hears the message about the kingdom and does not *understand* it.... But the one who received the seed that fell on good soil is the man who hears the word and *understands* it." Inside processing (making sense of or understanding) of outside information (the seed) is important.

Another Example

Perhaps you remember the occasion when Jesus was challenged by the Sadducees concerning a contrived narrative in which six brothers married, over time, the widowed wife of the first brother. They asked Jesus whose wife she would be in the resurrection. Each brother, following the custom of the day, had married in succession the widowed wife of the first brother who died, and each brother then died in succession after their marriage. (These events would bring a bit of suspicion in a court of law today!) Jesus replied, "Are you not in error because you do not know the Scriptures or the power of God?" (Mark 12:24). The Sadducees lacked knowledge. Jesus went on to teach them about marital relationship after the resurrection and about the resurrection as a demonstration of the power of God. He provided new information or new understanding to prior knowledge found in the Old Testament.

Jesus used a seemingly small thing to provide a major instruction. He reminded them that Moses recorded what God said to him at the burning bush: "I *am* the God of Abraham, the God of Isaac, and the God of Jacob" (Mark 12:26, emphasis mine). Jesus used a verb tense to declare that God is the God of the living and not the dead. Resurrection is possible because of the power of God. Then Jesus said, "You are badly mistaken!" (Mark 12:27). Humans can process incorrectly for lack of information, lack of good thinking habits, or even lack of desire. (The Sadducees may not have wanted to acknowledge the truth, since this was not a part of their belief system.) But the teacher, Jesus, provided additional **information** with evidence that they could choose to process and understand.

Outside information, as well as inside processing, is vital. Humans can be wrong because they lack information or because they have not connected or processed with accuracy. It is no wonder that God has given outside intervention to guide humans in the search for truth! We need help. Although God has given mankind the ability to reason, has created humans with the capacity to understand reality, and has provided His Word, we are still limited in our human capacity for complete understanding. We need help beyond our own construction of our own reality or truth. God has thus encouraged servant-leaders (pastors and teachers) to be "able to teach" (1 Timothy 3:2), and He has also provided the guidance of His Spirit.

There is a humbling awareness that, in the process of coming to know, there is a measure of subjectivity with sure limitations, but there is also a strong acknowledgement of the existence of objective truth that is knowable. For one who holds to a biblical worldview, reality and knowledge are public and verifiable by various ways of knowing, including God's revelation to humankind in His Word, in His son Jesus, and in His world. Christian scholars are seekers of truth, rather than creators of truth. As a teacher, I need to understand my role in the delivery of content, as well as understand the nature of knowing on the part of my students. Only a curriculum that considers both will maximize learning.

Implications for the Curriculum

The Christian, informed by a biblical worldview, must reject the postmodern epistemology (with denial of the objective existence of outside factors that impact learning) and determine the vital importance of content.

While the "progressive" side of the pendulum in the 100-year war has informed much of what we do related to *how humans learn*, particularly the active participation of the student in learning, the *nature of knowledge* has historically been better addressed by the traditionalist notion of objectivity. Therefore, the Christian worldview may not identify fully with either the "progressive" or "traditional" label. However, the third view of the nature of the student and learning and the nature of knowledge and knowing may serve us well.

The teacher must consider the "what" we learn along with the "how" we learn. The implications for one's developing philosophy of education, therefore, relate to these issues: (1) standards of knowledge vs. personally constructed knowledge, (2) assessment for understanding vs. self-assessment alone with little assessment of content, or the opposite, the assessment of parroted-back content/information alone, (3) truth as correspondence to reality vs. truth as a creation by the mind. Can you name other implications?

The teacher, then, understands that…

The student (knower) must be engaged (select, take in, intentionally process) using inside factors, such as prior knowledge, vocabulary, processing skills, etc.	}	Acknowledges inside factors
The content (information) available from outside the knower that exists in its own right.	}	Acknowledges outside factors

While plans and methodology for carrying out the plans are vitally important, a third element is crucial to a learning-centered curriculum. That element is the planned learning environment. Think about the kind of environment you wish to promote and develop. One way to explore this issue is to review the nature of the human and learning and ask, *What kind of environment is conducive to learning that mirrors what humans are like by nature? How can we work with the nature of the learner rather than against it?* Working with, not against, human nature makes learning easier for the student and much more rewarding. Review the role of the teacher and ask, *What are the factors involved in my role that will promote an optimal learning community?*

Activity | **The Planned Learning Community**

In my personal philosophy, I have labeled the environment that I like to promote as "relaxed structure." However, I unpack that label using the elements addressed above. Think through what you might say about the learning environment. Think through the implications for the classroom related to what you believe about each aspect of the learner as a special creation and image-bearer, a thinker, a chooser, an emotional and social creature, creative, communicative, etc. What might a Christian have to say about a loving, caring community in which the teacher is a model of Christ? (Refer to previous sections of your philosophy).

Write your thoughts here:

Activity | Write a Paragraph on the Nature of the Curriculum

You should now be ready to write a beginning paragraph on the nature of the curriculum. What is the nature of the curriculum in an educational (planned learning) setting, such as a school? Will it contain important content and skills? Will it include student processing activities? Will it include ongoing assessment? What will an effective learning environment or learning community look like? Why? You may wish to use these three categories.

Plans

Delivery

Environment

Write here:

12 | The Purpose of the Curriculum

Purpose of the Curriculum

When we address the purpose of the curriculum, we have come full circle. Beginning with the aim of education, we have moved through issues related to the nature of the student and learning, the role of the teacher in the learning event, and the nature of the curriculum. By now, it should be evident that there are interrelationships among all of the aspects of an educational philosophy. The philosophy document should be internally consistent and coherent and make sense as a useful whole integrated with one's root philosophy of life or worldview. It should also be an effective summary of beliefs that should impact practices. Best practices come from informed thought!

The purpose of the curriculum completes the circle by referring back to the aim of education, derived from the aim of life inherent in the foundational worldview being used by the educator. In our case, the worldview is Christian Theism.

Activity | Rewrite Your Aim of Education

Rewrite your understood aim of education informed by a Christian worldview. This will create a focus for identifying the purpose of the curriculum.

In chapter 4 of this book, I suggested one possible expression of an aim informed by a Christian worldview and the focus of Spears and Loomis in the book *Education as Human Flourishing*:

> While education does have utility, many educators believe that any utility derivable from education is secondary to higher and nobler ends. We live for truth, beauty and the achievement of proper conceptions of freedom. We also live for deeper relationships with others and a sustainable one with the created universe. We also live to know and understand God. Yes, choosing a vocation and getting a job are important by-products of an education. Yet the aim of a liberal education is to develop the mind and character in making choices between truth and error, between right and wrong (2009, p. 173).

An aim that reflects the thinking inherent in the paragraph above might read like this:

> **The aim of education is to promote human flourishing, the living out of what God intended His created image bearers to be:** by pursuing truth about God, His universe, and humankind (ourselves and others); by knowing, understanding, and effectively using knowledge and skills for wise living; and by acting ethically; thereby growing personally serving and benefiting society—all to the glory of God, the ultimate aim and first principal or *summum bonum* of LIFE!

How will you incorporate your stated aim of education into the purpose or "aim" of the curriculum in a Christian school?

Two Key Concepts in Curricular Design

Coherence and integration are current issues in school curricula found in many journals of curriculum theory, design, and development today. Perhaps you have heard of or studied multidisciplinary units, interdisciplinary learning, thematic units, and the integrated curriculum. These were buzzwords and innovations of the 1990s and earlier. In the mid-1990s, the Association of Supervision and Curriculum Development's Yearbook spoke directly to the issue of a coherent curriculum and what that should mean for human learning. We will explore the concept of "coherence" related to the curriculum and the relationship between a coherent curriculum and the purpose of the curriculum in a school setting. It will become apparent that the aim of education is achieved primarily through the *strategic design of the curriculum*. In other words, it is planned. It doesn't just happen! A Christian school does not fulfill its educational aim by simply enrolling students from Christian families, by hiring Christian teachers, or by adding a course in Bible to the curriculum. The Christian school curriculum is the key to a truly Christian education.

A Bit of History to Set the Stage

Curricular change is a given in America's schools. Change occurs almost yearly. More and more, change is apparent in schools around the globe, as well. I like to illustrate curricular change by highlighting the different ways a mathematics question has been asked over the past five or six decades. See if you can identify the curriculum issue and the purpose expressed by each of these tongue-in-cheek standardized test questions:

1960s arithmetic test: "A logger cuts and sells a truckload of lumber for $100. His cost of production is four-fifths of the amount. What is his profit?" Answer: $20

'70s new-math test: "A logger exchanges a set (L) of lumber for a set (M) of money. The cardinality of set M is 100. The set C of production costs contains 20 fewer points than set M. What is the cardinality of set P of profit?"

'80s "dumbed down" version: "A logger cuts and sells a truckload of lumber for $100. His cost is $80; his profit is $20. Find and circle the number 20."

'90s version: "An unenlightened logger cuts down a beautiful stand of 100 trees in order to make a $20 profit. Write an essay in your journal explaining how you feel about this way of making money."

21st century version: "A logger cuts and sells a truckload of lumber for $100. Because of high taxes on small businesses, his cost of production is a whopping four-fifths of that amount. What is his meager profit? And which of the new Common Core standards does this address?"

If you have studied the history of the American curriculum, you could probably identify the aims inherent in the curriculum just by the way the same basic math question was asked in this exaggerated account.

The curricular focus today, at least in theory, includes standards and core issues, as well as two concepts that have had staying power since the 1990s: integration and coherence. Those who promote intellectual coherence through the design of the curriculum believe that the school curriculum in America is fragmented and out of touch with the lives of students. They take the view that knowledge should be brought together into a unified body of knowledge for retrieval and use in decision-making, problem-solving, and enrichment and enjoyment in life. They understand that it is essential to have an integrating core around which (and out of which) to openly investigate, evaluate, and appreciate knowledge from various subject areas. This last view was highlighted in the book written in the late 1980s by Allan Bloom, *The Closing of the American Mind*. According to Bloom, a person must know something and believe something in order to have a touchstone by which to judge and evaluate new information. Those who believe everything, anything, or nothing tend to be closed-minded rather than truly open-minded. They cannot critically think and are stymied in their intellectual growth. Relativism is the only "truth" to them. Tolerance of all ideas as equal; "believe-everythingism" or "-anythingism" is the norm. Students have no way to judge what to bring into their belief system and what to discard; no way to critique what they are being taught; no way to determine the good, better, and best, and yes, the truth. Learning becomes absorption without critique. Bloom declared that this was the case for most of the students coming to the university in the late 1980s (Bloom 1987, pp. 36–41). His book was controversial, as you might imagine. His thoughts might apply to colleges and universities today as much as to high schools of yesteryear.

Just three years after Bloom's work, two social scientists from the Brookings Institute provided research that fortified Bloom's conclusion to some extent and triggered more controversy in the field of education. After studying the available research, John Chubb and Terry Moe concluded in the book *Politics, Markets, and America's Schools* that private schools were doing a better job than public schools in educating the youth of the nation. They reasoned that a private school does not have to be all things to all people. Among the conclusions they offered appeared the following, written about private schools:

> In the private sector, schools do not have to be all things to all people. To be successful, they need to find their niche—a specialized segment of the market to which they can appeal and attract support. The obvious way to do this is through the **strategic design of the curriculum** (p. 55, emphasis mine).

They go on to write about private schools.

Their goals are also more likely to have true intellectual **coherence** for they are not ad hoc

[handwritten: critical thinking: evaluating and considering new info in light of one's previous beliefs; judging based on one standard]

collections of value impositions, but packages that are consciously designed to constitute an integrated whole. The market allows and encourages its schools to have a distinctive, well-defined mission (p. 55, emphasis mine).

According to Chubb and Moe, the way that intellectual coherence occurs is through the "strategic design of the curriculum," planned to integrate and fulfill the mission of the school. It is targeted! It is planned! It is connected to the aim (mission) of education! Teachers must come to grips with this concept. The curriculum is the fleshing out of the aim of education and that aim should reinforce the aim of life.

While the goal of Chubb and Moe's book was not to promote private schools but rather to find the elements of the curriculum that would be powerful in helping the youth of America connect schooling to life in general, it was influential in the development of a hybrid sort of schooling, the charter school. Charter schools are public schools paid for with public money. Charter schools are usually under local administration and avoid a lot of state-directed red tape in their day-to-day functioning. They can, by design, fulfill some of the elements of a good education described by Chubb and Moe. They can have a more targeted mission than most general public schools, around which to organize learning (i.e. science or performing arts as the integrating core for the curriculum). Private schools can do even better.

While serving as president of the Carnegie Foundation for the Advancement of Teaching, at the same time period Chubb and Moe were conducting and presenting their findings, Ernest Boyer wrote the following on the "scholarship of integration":

> Schools need to create an environment that encourages students to…make connections across the disciplines, shape a more coherent view of knowledge and a more integrated, more authentic view of life (1990, p. 20).

Just five years later, the Association of Supervision and Curriculum Development, one of the most prestigious curriculum organizations in the world, commissioned a group of educators to address coherence and integration in the school curriculum. The title of the 1995 Yearbook was *Toward a Coherent Curriculum*. The book is a fascinating indictment of the fragmented curriculum and the lack of intellectual coherence that our youth face daily in the classrooms of America. The indictment included a charge that the current curriculum contributed to lack of connection between learning and life. It appears that many students agreed that "school is not

critical thinking allows students to think critically
and filters all info given
filter (God's word) it develops a worldview —

about my life!" (158). In all probability, they were in school "to get out," rather than to learn, or to be enriched, or to flourish as human beings. The writers of the Yearbook called for new approaches to integration and to determining the "glue" (or integrating core) that holds together the curriculum in such a way that students understand the relationship between school learning and all of life. The editor of the book, James Beane, writes,

> A coherent curriculum is one that holds together, that makes sense as a whole; and its parts, whatever they are, are unified and connected by the sense of the whole (1995, p. 3).

Notice the editor's conclusion: There is a need for a "glue" or integrating core. He continues:

> This kind of coherence will open up possibilities for the integration of educational experiences. That is, when the curriculum offers a sense of purpose, unity, relevance and pertinence—when it is coherent—young people are more likely to **integrate educational experiences into their scheme of meaning**, which in turn broadens and deepens the understanding of themselves and the world (1995, p. 4, emphasis mine).

Notice that in order for schooling and life to be integrated, there must be something that promotes coherence, the glue that holds the curriculum together:

> A search for coherence involves long-standing issues in the politics of curriculum because it must involve decisions about what ideas or themes will hold the curriculum together. The question of what the 'glue' is raises questions such as whose glue is it? Who decides what the glue is? (1995, p. 10)

By the end of the book, the editor asks a question and draws a conclusion: *Is it possible to reach consensus on the ideas, concepts, or goals that might hold the planned curriculum together?* The authors all agreed that curricular coherence is vital to learning, essentially the element that made school learning worthwhile. However, editor James Beane admitted that, because the integrating core, "glue," or "big ideas"—concepts, ideas, or goals, that might hold the planned curriculum together—are expressions of value, "it is worth asking whether it is possible to reach any kind of reasonable consensus regarding the possibilities of coherence" (1995, p. 175).

A tacit conclusion was that it is probably impossible to have a specific integrating core in public schools and real intellectual coherence may be elusive. Allan Bloom might agree with the sentiment that coherence may be elusive in an academic world that promotes relativism. What a sad conclusion! But not so for the Christian school or other private schools! Christian schools should know clearly the "glue" that holds the curriculum together and then design the curriculum for the promotion of intellectual coherence around that core. Indeed, biblical answers to life's biggest questions form "the knowledge most worth knowing" (as Spencer put it). For the Christian educator, a curriculum that is "rational" (Spencer's term) and makes sense as a unified whole will make possible the fulfillment of the aim of education, one that moves toward the development of human beings as God intended them to be as His image-bearers, functioning according to the pattern of human nature He designed, and experiencing the "good life" as a flourishing person who reflects His creatorship.

Intellectual Coherence Is a Function of Integration and Contributes to an Ongoing Integrated Life

At the university where I teach, we explore together three types of integration: (1) **subject-to-subject** integration, often called multi-disciplinary or interdisciplinary learning, thematic units and the like; (2) **subject-to-life** integration that includes authentic learning and assessment, which helps students to understand the connections between learning and life; and (3) **subject-to-worldview** integration, in the "strategic design of the curriculum," in which the teacher plans for the integration of biblical answers to life's biggest questions (a worldview approach) as the subjects of the curriculum are taught. The goal is that students view all of life and learning from God's perspective as a unified whole. Subject-to-subject and subject-to-life integration may be carried out in a public school classroom in the planning and delivery of the curriculum. Much has been written in recent years on multidisciplinary, interdisciplinary, and authentic learning. Worldview integration using a particular worldview is limited to private schools and home schools in America, at least in its robust form. Worldview pluralism by its nature and by law prohibits the integration of one specific worldview into the curriculum of public schools. Not so in private schools in the U.S.A. and around the world.

The section of your philosophy document referring to the purpose of the curriculum should describe your beliefs about these three types of integration, as well as the targeted result in the mind and life of the student that moves toward the fulfillment of the aim of education. In order to help the reader develop a working framework for the important task of biblical worldview integration, the last chapter of this book is a summary of the Integrating Core Approach to worldview integration that I developed and describe in *Undivided: Developing a Worldview Approach to Biblical Integration*, a suggested companion to this book. In the appendix section of this book, you will find an outline of the Integrating Core Model. We have been using this worldview approach in the development of a philosophy of education in this book, *By Design*.

Knowledge & knowing

Knowledge traditional   Knowing (created, knowledge)
                            progressive

Knowledge → is absolute

    Human is ~~create~~ an active creator
        of his own personal truth
↳ Human is a passive receiver of objective truth.
↳ we know no author & creative

objective : based on facts "unbiased"

Subjective: opinion → 'bias'

Coherence: quality of being consistent (common thread)
                biblical thred.

integration   process of bringing
                    together into a larger whole
(God is a God of order.

    Children should not purbe ohsurbing
        but filter, process, critique

    subject - to - subject   Math- science
    Subject - to - life   Language - History
    Subject - to -worldview

13 | Worldview Integration in the Design of the Curriculum

My Own Journey in the Development of Curricular Worldview Integration

I became involved in Christian Education in the early 1970s after graduating with a master's degree from a very fine Christian liberal arts college. My goal was to go back into the culture and impact people for Jesus Christ. My husband took a faculty position at Cairn University (then Philadelphia College of Bible), and I scheduled an interview for employment in the local public school. However, the day of the interview, I received a call from my pastor, who had started a Christian school several years earlier as a response to the court cases to remove prayer and Bible reading from the public schools. The key court case was waged in Abington, Pennsylvania, in the very school district in which I was seeking employment. The Christian school board offered me a teaching and part-time administrative position, and I took it.

After several weeks, I questioned myself, "What should I be doing differently here than I would be doing at the local public school?" I knew that parents wanted Bible reading and prayer as a part of their children's education, but there had to be something more. The journey for that something more led to the development of the model for biblical integration that I share in this book. Although no pedagogical models were available when I began, Christian educators were calling for biblical integration in the Christian schools. Some were also identifying biblical principles for each of the disciplines of knowledge. The secular-sacred divide, a dichotomy popular in the culture then and now, was negatively viewed by Christian educators and was a constant theme in seminars and workshops in the '70s. I listened to those pioneer thinkers and just began.

Background studies in the works of Christian philosopher Francis Schaeffer while I was a student at Wheaton College and my understanding of teaching and learning helped me to create student activities that would contrast and compare the content of the curriculum with the major issues in life identified and studied in philosophy. I used Jerome Bruner's concept of the T-chart as a strategy to compare and contrast concepts. My first attempts were clumsy, but enjoyable, and most of all seemed to be very much appreciated by the students. My approach, it seemed to me, was a philosophical or worldview approach. I found an interesting publication written by the Social Sciences Staff of the Educational Research Council, *The Human Adventure: Four World Views* (1971), which used a set of questions, called "controlling ideas." These questions were answered by each of the four worldviews addressed in the resource book: Traditional Chinese, Buddhists, Hebrews, and Greeks. I had my class add Christianity. Below are the questions from that curriculum:

1. What is the world and the universe?
   (What is it made of? How is it made? What can our senses tell us about it?)

2. What should human beings try to do with their lives?
   (Why are we here? What is our aim? What are our rights and duties?)

3. How can men and women know what is good and what is bad, or what is right and what is wrong?

4. Are human beings mainly good, or mainly bad, or a mixture of good and bad?

5. What is happiness? How can men and women find happiness?

6. Is there life after death?

7. Does God (or do gods) exist? ✳

8. Does God (or do gods) care about human beings?

9. Are any of the controlling ideas of this particular people shared with other people? Are some universally shared with all men and women? (p. 9)

The middle school curriculum often presented answers to these questions in various ways, and I looked for opportunities. The more I intentionally included biblical worldview integration into my curriculum, the more comfortable the planning became. I really did not need a pedagogical model as such. When I was asked, however, to speak at several Christian school conventions and conferences to share what I was doing, I was encouraged to put some effort into the development of an overall approach or pedagogy for biblical integration. Then, when I took a job in a college and had to teach future Christian school teachers the "how to" of worldview integration, I developed the model I currently use. In the last 15–20 years, other pedagogical models have been developed as well. It is encouraging to see men and women addressing this key issue today and contributing to the improvement of what we are doing in schools, particularly Christian schools.

Today, Biblical Worldview Integration Is a Basic Pedagogical Skill Being Developed by Christian School Teachers Worldwide

Not only do secular educators such as those cited earlier—James Beane, John Chubb and Terry Moe, and Allan Bloom—see the problems inherent in dividing a student's academic life into a secular-sacred dichotomy, but Christian educators and organizations that have been addressing the need for many years (such as the Association of Christian Schools International) are taking a very active role in providing models for teachers to use to accomplish the task. The concept of intellectual coherence produced by an integrated curriculum should be addressed in a philosophy of education informed by a biblical view of life and learning. The sacred-secular divide is alive and well in American culture, unknowingly impacting Christian educators who are not intentionally informed by their Christian worldview.

We are living and learning in a world with shifting and conflicting worldviews; this impacts learning. All students come to our schools with an already formed, but usually not intentionally informed worldview. The process of worldview integration is intentional and planned. There are several factors or elements to consider in the development of a biblical worldview in the strategic design of the curriculum. This is a curricular issue!

What Is a Worldview?

Simply put, a worldview is a set of beliefs that form a framework for making sense out of life and the world. These beliefs are the answers we hold to the basic questions of life that give meaning to everything we do. They help us understand who we are, why we are here, and where we are going. These answered questions form a perspective, a lens through which we view God, ourselves, the external world, everyday events such as life and death and ongoing history, knowledge, decision-making regarding right and wrong, and our destiny. We have been using a worldview approach in the development of our instructional philosophy in this book.

In *The Universe Next Door, A Worldview Catalog (5th Ed.)*, Sire describes a worldview as

> a commitment, a fundamental orientation of the heart, that can be expressed as a story or in a set of presuppositions (assumption which may be true, partially true, or entirely false) that we hold (consciously or subconsciously, consistently or inconsistently) about the basic constitution of reality, and that provides the foundation on which we live and move and have our being (p. 20).

Earlier editions of Sire's book described a worldview as a set of presuppositions or

> understandings or concepts that work to provide a coherent frame of reference for all of thought and action . . . A set of presuppositions or beliefs which we hold consciously or subconsciously about the basic make-up and meaning of the world and of life.

The Worldview Questions

The first aspect of curriculum development in which one intentionally designs biblical worldview integration is to answer worldview questions from a Christian Theistic position.

The first element is to determine what worldview issues or questions will be used as the framework for the integrating core. Early in my experience I used the controlling ideas found in the Educational Research Council social studies resource. When I discovered the first edition of *The Universe Next Door*, in the mid-1970s, I began to use the seven questions he uses to frame a worldview. They are very similar to those cited in the Educational Research Council book, so the development of the model was natural. Sire added an eighth question in his fifth edition. We introduced these questions when addressing the writing of your preamble and have been using them throughout as we integrate a biblical worldview with our developing philosophy of education. Here they are again:

1. What is prime reality—the really real? (the ultimate or starting reality, the foundation of one's worldview)

2. What is the nature of external reality, that is, the world around us?

3. What is a human being?

4. What happens to a person at death?

5. Why is it possible to know anything at all?

6. How do we know what is right and wrong?

7. What is the meaning of human history?

8. What personal life-orienting core commitments are consistent with this worldview? (life implications)

Differing worldviews answer these eight basic questions very differently, as you have seen through our examination of traditional and progressive philosophies and have contrasted and compared these to your own developing view.

A General Definition of Integration

Integration is the process of bringing together into a **larger whole**. More often than not, it is a process that connects or contrasts incoming knowledge with prior knowledge. How does this process fit with how the human learns by nature? An active-minded student hears or sees (feels, smells, tastes) by attending to incoming stimuli or information from the environment (teachers, textbooks, video, Internet, TV, DVD, friends, parents), then begins to make sense out of new knowledge and skills by using prior knowledge and experiences that are stored in memory. If there is no prior knowledge, the student may do a poor job of making sense out of the information. This is why teachers must engage the mind toward the lesson at hand by using student-friendly activities and experiences that connect to the life of the student.

This is true for biblical integration as much as for any other lesson in the curriculum. The student begins to process new incoming information to fit it in, make sense of it, and transform or change cognitive structures related to the new information. This is a process of bringing together into a larger whole. Something already there (or not there) inside the learner matters, as well as incoming information from outside. This is the heart of the concept of cognitive interactive learning as opposed to autonomously active or passive learning, and it is essential to understand this process for effective **development of a biblical worldview**.

The young Christian students we serve must have an integrating core (a set of beliefs) in order to enjoy, evaluate, and creatively use all of God's creation for His glory and His good pleasure. This core is also essential to the development of a flourishing human being, growing academically, personally, and spiritually. Worldview integration in a school setting addresses the whole person in a unified way that leads to a person of integrity (wholeness) who can impact his or her world for Christ. The word "integrity" comes from the same Latin root word, *integritas*, as does the word "integration." Literally, integrity means **wholeness**: being one person in public and in private, living in faithfulness to one set of principles whether or not anyone is watching. God's Word declares in the wisdom literature of Proverbs, "The integrity of the upright guides them, but the unfaithful are destroyed by their duplicity" (Proverbs 11:3). Biblical worldview integration that leads to intellectual coherence is vital in a Christian school in the development of the whole person.

The second aspect of curriculum development in which one intentionally designs biblical worldview integration is to understand how the process of integration fits with how humans learn (already a part of your philosophy) and then to make sure that curricular lessons are built upon that knowledge.

When a teacher uses good cognitive interactive lessons and uses subject-to-subject and subject-to-life activities (many of which can be found in curriculum materials today), it becomes much easier to intentionally plan ways to have the students process and internalize the answers to worldview questions as an *integral part* of the regular curriculum. In the planning, the teacher creates student processing activities designed to help students think through, from a biblical perspective, the content of the lessons and units—whether the visual and performing arts, the language arts, the natural and social sciences, history, mathematics, or physical education. Biblical integration is not the same as a devotional or prayer at the beginning of class. It is not required chapel each week. It is not just the Bible curriculum in the Christian school. It is a process that leads to intellectual coherence and frames the entire school curriculum!

In his book *Engaging God's World: A Christian Vision of Faith, Learning and Living*, Cornelius Plantinga writes about bringing all of the parts of life—including education—under the lordship of Christ. He writes in this case about higher education, but his thoughts are applicable to all Christian education:

> No matter how a Christian college plans to integrate faith, learning, and service, it will never just conduct education-as-usual—not if it is serious about Christian higher education. It won't even do education-as-usual with Bible classes tacked on, or education-as-usual with prayers before class, or education-as-usual with a service-learning component and a 10 o'clock chapel

break. No, a solidly Christian college will rise from its faith in Jesus Christ and then explore the height and depth, the length and breadth of what it means to build on this faith.… For a lifetime of learning and work within the kingdom of God (p. xiv).

Character Education as Biblical Integration

So often, I find that Christian schools have a curriculum for character development that they consider their biblical integration aspect of the curriculum. Character education is wonderful. However, character education is just a third of worldview integration (axiology or questions about values). Furthermore, although character education addresses biblical characteristics such as love, kindness, patience with others, compassion and forgiveness, it is not necessarily the best way to address essential questions about values. The question, "How do we know the difference between good and bad, right and wrong, etc.?" is best answered for the Christian by studying and knowing the character of God, not just social conventions for the classroom or society. Character education, to be considered part of the process of worldview integration, should intentionally help to answer the worldview question concerning how we know right and wrong, connecting the aim of human character to the standard for the good: the character of God Himself.

A Class or Course in Bible as Biblical Integration

Bible teaching or a separate curricular class for Bible is sometimes viewed as the biblical integration part of the school curriculum. Bible teachers are vital in a school's attempts to do biblical worldview integration. However, while the biblical facts, names, places, and chronology of events are very important, lessons should also be aimed at answering major questions of life. As an example, take the wonderful story of Joseph in Genesis 39–50. It holds many biblical truths to be considered, but often a worldview issue is missed by those Bible teachers who focus on facts and chronology alone or focus on typologies (Joseph as a type of Christ), or those who separate the story into so many sub-stories that the big idea is missed. When this is the case, teachers miss opportunities to expose students to answers to worldview questions. They must be aware of what their part is in the overall process. Here is a helpful approach to planning a Bible lesson or unit for Bible teachers: *planning lessons*

1. Study the Bible passage and read out the main idea or big idea. Highlight the relevant events, verses, cross references, etc.

2. Formulate a target understanding and student response, and convert these into instructional and response objectives.

3. Ask: "How will I know that the student understands and can envision response?" Write a tentative assessment activity, scenario, or question. (This is a form of UbD—Understanding by Design or backward planning design.)

4. Ask: **"What worldview question(s) is/are addressed in this lesson?"** (This is often missed by Bible teachers.) *How would we see this today,*

5. Design a motivation activity to engage the mind toward the truth to be learned. When possible, use the prior knowledge and experiences of the student.

6. Provide a way for the student to receive the new information: guided inductive study or "read to find out" activity, storytelling, lecture, DVD of story, paraphrased reading/writing, etc.

7. Student processing activities. What can I have the student do to help promote understanding and envision response? How can the students fit in the new information with previous knowledge, their own life experience, and their developing Christian worldview?

8. Add or modify the assessment already planned.

Illustration: Life of Joseph

Big Idea or Bible truth to be learned:

God can use both the good and bad circumstances/events in our lives for our good and His good purposes; we can trust Him.

Objective:

The student will be able to explain God's sovereign work in a human life using the life of Joseph and other related passages.

Response to the truth to be learned (aim):

The student will trust God to work all things in his life for good.

Worldview question(s):

Who is prime reality? God is.

What kind of a God is He? He is a personal God who intervenes in the affairs of humans and can be trusted. He can take both the good and the bad circumstances and use them for good.

Who is in control of history (personal, national, universal)? A sovereign God who is working out His plan and purposes.

The worldview question in the life of Joseph is answered in Genesis 50:15–21. To his brothers who thought Joseph would seek revenge after the death of his father, Joseph said, "You intended to harm me, but God intended it for good to accomplish what is now being done, the saving of many lives. So then, don't be afraid." Romans 8:28 is a generalization of this truth and a good verse to memorize. Bible teachers, including self-contained classroom teachers who teach Bible, have a vital role in helping to form the knowledge-base for biblical integration that will be done in the other disciplines of study in the school curriculum. It will work two ways: knowledge gained and understood in Bible class will enhance integrative activities in other subject areas, while knowledge in other subject areas and the mental habit of worldview integration will enhance the knowledge gained in Bible class. The entire curriculum in the Christian school must be integrative.

Regarding the phenomenon of learning this way, J. P. Moreland claims that the more one knows the more one can "see" (perceive) with understanding:

> We often read the Bible, hear the news, listen to a sermon, or talk to friends yet we don't get much out of it. One central reason for this may be the lack of knowledge and intellectual growth. The more you know, the more you see and hear because your mind brings more to the task.... In fact, the more you know about extrabiblical matters, the more you will see in the Bible. Why? Because you will see distinctions in the Bible or connections between Scripture and an issue in other areas of life that would not be possible without the concepts and categories placed in the mind's structure by gaining the relevant knowledge in these extrabiblical areas of thought. Thus, general intellectual development can enrich and contribute to Bible study and spiritual formation (1997, p. 79).

Subject-to-Worldview Integration

Moreland's words are a good segue into looking at worldview integration in the subject areas of the curriculum other than Bible. In the integrating core model, the teacher must move from his or her examined biblical worldview to the new knowledge to be taught, intentionally looking for natural, unforced opportunities to bring together, correlate, and correct ("connections" and "distinctions" in Moreland's terms) the concepts and facts presented in the curriculum with biblical answers to worldview questions that might be addressed. The process of integration will serve to enhance the student's growing worldview and the use of that worldview in life outside the classroom by helping to develop the student's skills of critical thinking. The designed curricular activities not only teach the subject content with integrity but also shed light on the issues by incorporating a biblical perspective. Therefore, the student will develop intellectual coherence, be enriched and appreciative of new learning, and be able to challenge a nonbiblical assumption or conclusion. While this may seem somewhat idealistic to many Christian teachers, it is the goal of integration. There are many educators who would argue that integration of the school curriculum is not only necessary for intellectual coherence but also good for the human personality. Armand Nicholi argued that, when it is a biblical view, such as that of C. S. Lewis after his conversion, it serves to help one view life in a more healthy way. It is a worthy goal!

The Integrating Core Pedagogical Model

See Outline of Elements—Appendix Two

The model I have developed and used for more than 35 years is one I call the *Integrating Core Model*. This model begins with a whole—the integrating core—a set of examined worldview beliefs that are more than the stories learned in Sunday school or nice Christian feelings or God-words that are sometimes repeated as Christian mantras, such as "What would Jesus do?" or "If you love Jesus, you wouldn't…" Rather, the core is comprised of biblical truths that address life's biggest questions, including questions about being or existence (the existence of God, human beings, and the created world), questions about knowledge and knowing, and questions about values (the good and beautiful, the bad and the ugly, right and wrong, character, and the core commitments and values in life). Conceptually, the model may be diagrammed like this:

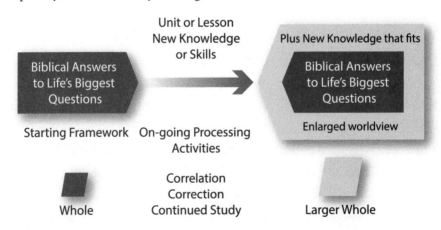

As a curricular* visual, the model may be depicted as below:

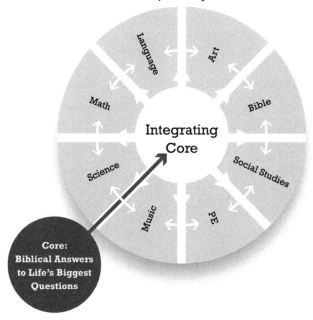

* *Curriculum* comes from the Latin word for *course*, as in race course, and is often depicted in circular designs.

There are three types of student processing activities planned in the curriculum: **connections** (correlation), **distinctions** (correction in light of a biblical view), and **continued study**. Student processing activities are an integral part of the curriculum unit or lesson, challenging students to examine God's perspective on science, math, language arts and literature—whatever the subject at hand. The teacher must also assess worldview integration in the mind of the student, just as he or she would assess any learning. This may mean writing a test question, preparing a project assignment or activity, or requiring a performance of some kind to measure worldview connections and distinctions with biblical understandings. It will be helpful to add to your lesson preparation a worldview integrative objective that will guide both your assessment and your methodology.

The curricular lesson might lead to the necessity of designing continued study in a direction that will ultimately allow for student integrative activities. This is especially the case when an issue emerges in class for which the teacher had not planned as a part of the curricular activities. If there is no immediately applicable answer from either the subject area or God's Word, the teacher should plan with the students how to investigate the issue.

Developing a curriculum that includes biblical worldview integration is an application that grows out of one's educational philosophy, especially out of one's view of the aim of education. The purpose for the curriculum spells out how that aim is accomplished through the strategic design of the curriculum.

How do we develop students who are flourishing as human beings, people of integrity (wholeness), rather than students who manifest duplicity, instantly secular or instantly sacred on demand (a divided worldview)? How do we contribute to the growth of intellectual coherence in our students? How do we help students to develop integrated, rather than disintegrated, personalities? How do we help to develop students and educators who will reflect their Creator in all they do in life (including their vocation) and in learning? I firmly believe that curricular biblical worldview integration is the GPS (Global Positioning System) that will help to get us there.

Issues to Consider Integral to the Process of Integration and Your Developing Philosophy of Education

Prior beliefs of the student matter.

One important factor to consider is what students already believe to be true and the limits of their vocabulary and previous experiences. We cannot assume that students have mentally stored biblical truths by which they can automatically connect new information. However, we can assume that they have in their minds a combination of biblical truths, partial truths, or misconceptions as judged by biblical truth. Integrative activities will, on the one hand, enrich and fortify their developing worldview and, on the other hand, clarify and correct misconceptions. Can you see how this relates to the nature of the human and learning addressed in your philosophy of education?

> Something already there or not and new information work together in learning. This is the primary principle of this pedagogical approach to biblical worldview integration.

Prior knowledge and an already developing worldview are illustrated in the words of a young boy after the death of his father. When John Lennon was shot in 1980, his son, Sean, was interviewed by a reporter who recorded his words in the local newspaper. When asked about his daddy, the young child said to the reporter something like: "Now my daddy is everything; everything is my daddy; my daddy is god."

I thought at the time that this was evidence for the development of a child's worldview, the content of which had been assimilated into the cognitive structures of the mind and was ready to be expressed in life (and death) situations. If the words of the reporter were truly Sean's, they indicate an already-developing worldview. Although the boy had not yet examined and systemized his views, he had a developing Pantheistic worldview, perhaps taught to him by his parents, John Lennon and Yoko Ono. Our students are no different, except for the immediate environment and worldview in which they have been immersed. They come to us with an already developing worldview that needs to grow and be examined.

Students must process biblical truth with heart and mind.

Promoting a biblical worldview must be more than presenting a devotional thought, lecture, or biblical thought to our students. In order to prepare our youth to live out their connected worldview, student processing integrative activities must be written into the curriculum. The activities should lead students to compare and contrast, connect, relate, distinguish, correct, or continue to study subject matter as it is impacted by biblical answers to life's biggest issues. The worldview answers are not just the teacher's view, but God's. This is vital in this day and age of mantras such as "This is my truth" and "That's truth to you but not to me." Objective truth is dead among so many youth today. Our young people are strongly predisposed to relativism and openness to thinking that all truths are equally valid and therefore, none should have the status as "truth."

Young people turn off even beloved teachers when they begin to "preach" at them at the end of a lesson in science or social studies, or when teachers tell them that they should listen and learn this biblical principle because this truth has "worked for me." Students need to grapple with issues and draw conclusions under the guidance of one who knows and loves the Lord, who will gently lead them toward God's perspective through activities that require comparing and contrasting, correlating and correcting, and drawing conclusions. When understood and connected to life issues and the disciplines of learning, God's Word will lead students to develop a knowledge-base for current and future integration and decision-making. This base will not be just the second-hand knowledge of the teacher or school but rather be internalized and understood as an integral part of their own schema of meanings. They will develop the categories in the mind to truly know God's perspective on key issues in learning and life, which will, in turn, broaden and deepen their understanding of themselves, others, the universe, and God. Hopefully, in a community of believers (family, church, Christian school) they will develop a healthy disposition toward thinking and walking in God's ways and loving Him with mind and heart. A **heart** for God predisposes **knowing about** God and **knowing** God Himself.

Conclusion

How *should* we view our scholarly activity related to becoming a teacher or school administrator? How should our educational philosophy inform our practices?

A teacher who views instructional philosophy from God's perspective will view every student as one created in the image of God; able to think, feel, choose, and create; designed and created to reflect the God of the universe; a special creation of incredible worth, yet marred by a flawed nature because of the Fall of mankind. But the teacher will also view each student as one who can experience the love, grace, and mercy of a personal, relational God who offers redemption in Christ and restoration of all He intended for humans to be as image-bearers. Compare the view above to the perspective of some that humans are merely machines or highly complex animals with no qualitative difference from the animal kingdom, or to the view that humans are sleeping gods that need only to remember their lofty state as gods. Worldview issues matter!

A teacher's overall approach to teaching will be informed by an understanding of human nature and learning. Christian teachers who are informed by a biblical worldview will not only study well and know their subjects, but will also know their students and promote learning in a way that helps students process and internalize new information into their schemas of meaning using their God-given capacity to learn. If teachers believe that students are cognitively interactive, they will understand the importance of outside factors (such as, the content, materials, the environment, and their preparedness as a teacher), as well as inside factors that come with each student learner. Compare the cognitive interactive approach above to a view based on the belief that humans are cognitively passive in the learning event. These teachers use a telling, testing, and reinforcing-with-stickers-and-grades approach that so often leads to quickly forgotten information or the inability to retrieve and use the information in a variety of ways. On the other side of the pendulum swing, compare the view of interactive learning to the approach of the teacher who believes that everything comes from inside the students, who learn by the promptings of their own interests and their own personal activity, making specific content relatively unimportant.

Integrated Christian educators will view their role, first and foremost, as promoters of student learning. They are hired to teach so that students learn. Secondarily, they will view their role as teachers who model a nonmoving target, the Lord Jesus Christ, whose compassion, love, and forgiveness we are instructed to imitate and model. Compare that view to one that holds that the teacher is not a role model at all, or to one that thinks the teacher ought to model the ideal citizen according to current standards of the culture. Thirdly, in classroom management and discipline, Christian teachers understand that what they do is for the "good of the child" and not to prove their own power. They will never view themselves as the "boss" but as one with delegated authority: a servant leader. The goal is that students, my students, whether in first grade or college, will see learning and life as an integral whole, the foundation for which is a biblical worldview that answers life's biggest questions. The view of the teacher matters!

Write and Edit Your Philosophy Informed by the Integrating Core of a Biblical Worldview

You are now ready to write and edit your own personal philosophy of education informed by a Christian worldview. May it be more than a dusty old paper that sits in some teacher's file, or part of a faculty file of résumés in a school office, or a computer file that is never really fleshed out or used in your teaching. May it be a document that, while open to modification over time, will serve to make you a more consistent, coherent teacher or administrator who clearly thinks and acts in accordance with a biblical view of life and learning.

At the end of this study and writing activity, you should begin to condense, remove redundancy, and polish your document. Your written philosophy has now been examined and systematized and intentionally informed by your biblical worldview. There should be no pressure to word your thinking in any special way for employment in a public school or a Christian school. This latter concern is part of writing for an audience and may, of course, be addressed later. For now, just get your thinking down on paper in your own words. This is your personal philosophy informed by your worldview and is (probably) not for publication at this point (unless a professor asks for it). It is for mental digestion and use.

A conclusion of no more than two or three sentences will complete the document. Referring back to the aim of education as it impacts the purpose of the curriculum is a good way to conclude the document. The writing is in your hands.

I Conclude with a Personal Note

My husband put a little book on my desk a few years ago with a title that took me aback: *Fit Bodies, Fat Minds* (Os Guinness). I had a reasonably "fit body" at the time, but I wondered whether my husband was intimating that I had a "fat head"! I had to know. So I opened it immediately. The first thing that hit my sight upon opening the book was a cartoon. I love to use cartoons and never skip these in books. This one depicted a challenge of the day in which we live: People (specifically Christians as I later read) often have great bodies (firm buttocks the cartoon actually read) but "silly putty" brains. Guinness was actually writing on the lost art of using the human mind for God's glory, not as an elite intellectualism to simply replace the seemingly anti-intellectualism pervading the evangelical world in America, but rather using the mind as faithfulness to the commands of Jesus. Guinness writes:

> Our lament is not for the destruction of the elite culture of Western civilization but for the deficiencies in our everyday discipleship as Christians. Our mission is not the recovery of some lost golden age of purportedly better Christian thinking but the renewal of the church today that has integrity, faithfulness, and effectiveness in its thinking. Once again, thinking Christianly is first and foremost a matter of love—of minds in love with God and the truth of His world (p. 19). *Permanecer en Él.*

Guinness ends his introduction to the book by remarking, "To the extent God has given us minds, we must love God with all our minds and in all of our lives in a way that is shaped decisively by Him" (p. 21). To which I say: "Amen!" To intentionally develop a philosophy of education informed by a Christian worldview falls, I believe, into the category of thinking Christianly as a matter of love for God and the truth of His Word and His world. May our minds as educators be shaped by Him.

Summary of Some of the Philosophies of Education Held in the Twenty-First Century

	Perennialism	Essentialism	Behaviorism	Progressivism	Educational Humanism	Reconstructionism
Root General Philosophy	Neo-Scholasticism	Idealism, Realism	Realism	Pragmatism	Neo-Pragmatism, Existentialism	Neo-Pragmatism, Postmodernism
Educational Aim	Understandings of great ideas of Western civilization; Train the intellect (mind); moral development; serve the society	Acquire basic skills/knowledge for survival and contribution to society as a good citizen; moral education	Acquire behaviors that will lead to a good society	The whole child. Develop the ability to function in society and to problem solve	Development of the individual self for living a satisfying life; healthy whole persons lead to healthy societies	Examine institutional status of marginalized groups; take social action; Fix society using the schools
Curriculum	Emphasis on enduring ideas: truths which are constant and unchanging, especially learned through the classics; Cultivation of the mind: history, literature, religion, philosophy	Emphasis on basic skills: reading, writing and arithmetic; Essential common core of basics; information and skills needed for living and citizenship	Emphasis on science and math; world of the observable is ultimate reality and worth knowing; determine the knowledge and skills needed and condition them or discover them	Emphasis on problem solving and useful skills; Derived from student interests that are student initiated; Active experimentation; Social experience; focus on society	Emphasis on processes and experiences that are student initiated; creativity; choice; focus on individual	Emphasis on works of marginalized people (multicultural issues, feminine issues, and other underrepresented groups); Solve social problems; promote diversity; create new world order or better society

A2 | Developing the Integrating Core Model

Today, many people use the term *worldview* in everyday conversation. Christian pollsters and writers have polled the Christian community to see whether or not evangelical Christians have an informed worldview that impacts their thinking and practice. Findings indicate that many Christians divorce their everyday lives from a biblical perspective, while still giving lip service to biblical Christianity on Sunday, Christmas, and Easter, at weddings and funerals, and when tragedy strikes. This dualistic practice is not consistent with the description of a worldview as a coherent framework for thought and action, nor with the definition of integrity and integration as wholeness, nor is it consistent with the assumed goal of a Christian school or Christian institution of higher education.

In my view, the mission of Christian schools everywhere should be to help students develop a worldview informed by biblical answers to life's biggest questions. The desired outcome is a student whose perspective is God's perspective in all areas of inquiry—the natural sciences, mathematics, the language arts, the visual and performing arts, social studies, and physical education. This is a curricular issue.

Why Is Worldview Integration So Vital to School Education?

Intellectual coherence requires a view of knowledge as a unified whole, rather than fragmented and segmented bits and pieces of subject matter committed to memory for a test and then forgotten, or a course title and passing grade on a transcript. Those who promote intellectual coherence consider it essential to have an integrating core around which and out of which to openly investigate, evaluate, and appreciate knowledge from various subject areas.

Integrating Core Model

Developed by Marti MacCullough, EdD

Below is a basic outline of the elements of the Integrating Core model. There are four major elements in the approach:

1. Worldview questions answered by a biblical worldview

2. Engaging, cognitive interactive lessons (instructional objectives, engaging motivation, new information or skills, student processing activities for the lesson, assessment)

3. Designed student processing activities—connections (correlations), distinctions (corrections), and continued study

4. Assessment of worldview objective

Describing the Elements

Element One: Biblical answers to life's biggest questions

My students are required to read and chart all the different worldviews cataloged in Sire's book *The Universe Next Door* and compare them to Christian Theism. For example, Sire's third question is, "Who or what is a human being?" Answers vary by worldviews that might hold that a human is a machine, an animal, a sleeping god, a naked ape, or a person made in the image of God.

The teacher must know and understand the issues addressed by a biblical worldview, then use this knowledge in the process of integration. Using a framework such as the questions in Sire's book helps to make the task manageable. Working together in planning groups and sharing ideas is also constructive for Christian school faculties that wish to begin to use integrative activities. This approach is far less intimidating than asking each Christian teacher to become a theologian or insisting that only trained Bible teachers can do biblical worldview integration. All growing Christian school teachers should be able to articulate biblical answers to major questions of life and to identify contrary views. Of course, some will understand more and should be willing to help fellow teachers. Biblical worldview integration is a community affair in a Christian school. The entire school is involved.

Element Two: Engaging, interactive lessons

Although this book is not about learning theory per se, it must be said that true worldview integration cannot be accomplished in a classroom in which students are spoon-fed material and not encouraged to process, make sense out of new knowledge, and draw conclusions. Students must be engaged mentally and challenged to use prior knowledge to connect and fit new knowledge into their existing schemas so that they can store and retrieve knowledge for use in real life and not just to give it back in rote fashion for an A on a test. Vital to these connections are student processing activities that require critical thinking, judging and evaluating based upon a standard and drawing conclusion. Also, subject-to-subject integration and subject-to-life integrative activities (the kind of activities now appearing in many published curriculum materials) are tremendous helps in engaging the mind toward subject-to-worldview integration.

Element Three: Student processing activities

The processing activities for worldview integration can be categorized into three types and may be planned in any part of the lesson. The three types are:

1. Connection, or correlation, or comparison—What in the lesson today or in this unit correlates or connects or fits together with a biblical view?

2. Distinction, or correction, or contrast—What in the lesson today or in the unit needs to be evaluated in light of biblical answers to worldview questions or issues because it *appears* to conflict with what we know clearly from God's Word?

3. Continued study—A third type of processing activity may occur when something in the lesson today brings up a question in the mind of the student or teacher for which there is no immediate answer from either the subject area or the Bible. This question presents an opportunity to experience further study together. (I used to call this type of processing activity "conflict," rather than "continued study"; however, I found that usually the questions do not really represent conflict but rather a lack of knowledge and understanding about a topic.)

The above activities must be written into the regular curriculum.

Examples of Three Types of Student Processing Activities
at the Basic Education Level

Connection, correlation, distinction, correction

Many years ago, when I first began to biblically integrate, I was substituting for a second-grade teacher. One of the stories in the second-grade reader was about a little Indian boy (Native American) who had been born sickly. He could not go to regular school. He was homebound. In the story, the grandfather tells the boy that his name means "strength" and he tells him that if he repeats his name over and over, all will be well. It was a beautiful story of a grandfather's love. However, at the end of the story, the classroom teacher is encouraged to have the students take note of the last line of the story: "Isn't it wonderful that we have the gift of language to talk to ourselves in time of need?"

I had very little time to prepare, but quickly saw possibilities for integration. We *did* discuss the wonderful gift of language given to humans created in the image of God to communicate our thoughts to others and to God. We *did* ask why God would choose to speak to humans using written language in the form of a book. (Even second graders can correlate and draw conclusions.) This activity was correlative/connective.

I then asked the class what they thought about the last sentence and whether or not they might have a better idea. One little boy raised his hand and replied, "Mrs. MacCullough, when I get hurt or when I am sick, I don't talk to myself. I talk to my mommy." We took time to thank God for our moms. Reminded by our prayer of thanks, another little boy said, "We can talk to God, too, just like now." That comment started a good discussion on communicating with God. Finally, I asked the class what they might do to encourage and show love and care for a child who is homebound. Their suggestion to send notes of encouragement were followed by an activity of writing notes to a real child in their class who had been out sick for a while. On the notes the students wrote, "We are *talking* to God and asking Him to make you better." This was connective. Compassion and love are qualities of Christ-likeness. The concepts of prayer and good deeds are biblical worldview issues. They help to answer the questions, "What kind of God is our God?" and "What kind of people should we be?" The answers we discovered were,

• "A personal God who hears and answers prayer."

- "He communicates and so do we. We use language to talk to God and to others."

- "How do we know right and wrong? God's character is the measure of goodness and He asks us to love, care for, and encourage one another. We can use language to do this."

Example of Continued Study

An example of "continued study" might serve to make this type of planned study understood. In the 1970s, I started a program for gifted children in the Christian school in which I taught. One day in the course of discussion, one gifted student asked a question that led to a month of continued study. He said, "Mrs. MacCullough, this book says that 70 million years before man walked on this planet, dinosaurs died out. The Bible says that on the sixth day of creation all beast and creeping things and man were created. My pastor said so. How do you explain that?" (There was a bit of disequilibrium—mine!)

I did not have an answer. I did have some vague notions about the views and interpretations of Genesis 1 and 2. Up to that time, I had done little research on dinosaurs, although my students had mastered dinosaur data. What a surprising and wonderful month of activities! The activities branched out into my regular sixth grade classroom and I learned so much about the dinosaur family. We ended up measuring a section of the school parking lot and on down the street block to determine the size of Noah's ark, which we then compared with the Nina, Pinta, and Santa Maria. (This was an example of interdisciplinary biblical integration with mathematics.) My students (and I) were overwhelmed by the size of the ark. One student had wondered whether or not a dinosaur or two could have fit on the ark if they were still alive when Noah was around. Two gifted students calculated the volume of the ark and determined that two dinosaurs, even pretty big ones, could fit with room to spare. Of course, this was speculative, but we were not being closed-minded. We compared the ratio of the ark to the accepted ideal ratio of seafaring ships. My pastor, a former Philadelphia shipyard worker volunteered to visit my class when he heard what we were doing. He shared that modern ships (including the Titanic) use the ratio God built into the dimensions of the ark. My kids were surprised that God is so smart. I know this because one of the students said, "Wow, God is smart!" This is worldview integration: "What kind of God is He? He is smart!"

This one continued study activity led to several other projects, including some fun activities designed to understand the dinosaur family and to appreciate these extinct creatures as the creation of God. I did not want to follow in the footsteps of the orthodox Jews in Jerusalem, who threatened to boycott a milk company for putting pictures of dinosaurs on cartons of milk, because dinosaurs were a sign of evolution. One Jewish head of family admitted that when he purchased an encyclopedia, he cut out all of the parts that did not fit with his religion. That, in my view, is intellectual suicide, not intellectual coherence! If dinosaurs existed (and they did) they are God's creation and need to be studied in light of His perspective, even if some of what we study is speculative in nature!

Illustration from the University Level

My educational psychology course has ample natural opportunities for worldview integration. The key questions in educational psychology are "What is a human being?" and "How do humans develop and learn?" Worldview questions at stake are found in each of the three philosophical issues: *metaphysical* (What is a human being? Is there a God, and if so, what kind of God is He?), *epistemological* (How do humans know/learn? Can we know reality? What is knowledge?), and *axiological* (How do we develop our self-concept as valued persons? How do we develop morally deciding right and wrong? How do we determine beauty?). These are just a few of the issues addressed. Some of these have been addressed in this book as you have been asked to stop, research, think, and write.

When addressing and exploring learning theories that hold to the active, passive, or interactive actional views of the nature of human beings, we explore which of these views fits best with a biblical view of the human being. Students are grouped and instructed to research evidence in Scripture to determine and defend their views. Groups then share their conclusions with the class and these conclusions are discussed and challenged. Multiple views on Constructivism are addressed and evaluated using the underlying assumptions related to knowing.

Additional examples of worldview integrative student activities may be found in the companion book, *Undivided: Developing a Worldview Approach to Biblical Integration*.

Element Four: Assessment Activities

These activities are designed to evaluate learning and more specifically worldview integration. They are similar to good assessment activities used on a daily basis by effective teachers. Use of the expressive language arts, writing and speaking activities and assignments, are good for assessing worldview integration. In the aforementioned educational psychology class, students are required to develop their own theory of learning, beginning with their underlying assumptions related to the nature of the human being and learning and the nature of knowledge and knowing, much like you have been doing as you have written your philosophy of education. Your written philosophy of education with all parts informed by your Christian worldview will be the assessment for this book.

Conclusion

Developing biblical worldview integration in the strategic design of the curriculum takes every bit as much work for classroom teachers as the most important lesson or unit currently taught to bring about an important learning outcome. This approach to integration takes preparation and planning, study and commitment. It takes a pedagogical model and practice. But it is very worthwhile.

(Paper)
- intro chns.
- aim of ed.
- nature of learner

spiritual, physical, intellectual

- Role of the teacher
  purpose of the curriculum.

   3 elem. of Ed

Nature Student

Role teacher = 4 wayne can categoriz
                their work

purpose curriculum

R | **References**

Adler, M. 1985. *Ten philosophical mistakes*. New York: MacMillan Publishing Company.

Arum, R. 2003. *Judging school discipline: The crisis of moral authority*. Boston: Harvard University Press.

Baum, L. F. 1900. *The wonderful wizard of Oz*. Chicago, IL: George M. Hill Company.

Beane, J. A., ed. 1995. *Toward a coherent curriculum, the 1995 yearbook of the Association of supervision and curriculum development*. Alexandria, Virginia: ASCD Press.

Bigge, M. & S. Shermis. 2004. *Learning theories for teachers: An Allyn & Bacon Classics Edition*. 6th Ed. Boston: Pearson Education, Inc.

Bloom, A. 1987. *The closing of the American mind*. New York: Simon and Schuster.

Boyer, E. 1990. *Scholarship reconsidered: priorities of the professoriate*. Princeton, New Jersey: The Carnegie Foundation for the Advancement of Teaching.

Bruner, J. 1960. *The Process of Education*. Cambridge, Mass.: Harvard University Press.

Braley, J., J. Layman, & R. White, eds. 2003. *Foundations of Christian School Education*. Colorado Springs, CO: Purposeful Design.

Chopra, D. 1992. *Escaping the prison of the mind: A journey from here to here* [audiobook edition]. San Rafael, CA: New World Library,

Chubb, J. E. & T. Moe. 1990. *Politics, markets, and America's schools*. Washington, D.C.: The Brookings Institute.

Clark, G. 1981. *A Christian view of men and things*. Grand Rapids: Baker Book House.

Comenius, J. A. 1896. *Comenius' school of infancy: An essay on the education of youth during the first six years*. W. S. Monroe, ed. Boston: D.C. Heath.

Creed, L. & M. Masser. 1985. The greatest love of all [Recorded by Whitney Houston]. On *Whitney Houston* [CD]. Los Angeles, CA: Arista Records.

design. 2012. In Merriam-Webster.com. Retrieved December 13, 2012, from http://www.merriam-webster.com/dictionary/design

Doll, W. E., Jr. 1993. *A post-modern perspective on curriculum*. New York: Teachers College Press.

Froebel, F. 1906. *The education of man*. (W. N. Hailmann, A.M., Trans.). New York, NY: D. Appleton and Company. (Original work published 1887).

Ginott, H. 1973. *Teacher and child: A book for parents and teachers*. New York: The Macmillian Company.

Goleman, D. 1987, August 25. Embattled giant of psychology speaks his mind. *The New York Times*. Retrieved from http://www.nytimes.com/1987/08/25/science/embattled-giant-of-psychology-speaks-his-mind.html?pagewanted=all&src=pm

Guiness, O. 1994. *Fit bodies, fat minds: Why evangelicals don't think and what to do about it*. Grand Rapids: Baker Books.

Hargreaves, A., ed. 1997. *Rethinking educational change with the heart and mind*. Alexandria: VA: Association for Supervision and Curriculum Development.

Hart H., van der Hoeven, J., & N. Wolterstorff. 1983. *Rationality in the Calvinian tradition.* Toronto, Canada: University Press of America.

Hoang, C. 2012, May 21. Revolution from within: Improving self-esteem with Gloria Steinem [Blog post]. Retrieved from https://continuousprojectaltereddaily.wordpress.com/2012/05/21/revolution-from-within-improving-self-esteem-with-gloria-steinem/

Hutchins, R. M. 1943. *Education for freedom.* Baton Rouge, Louisiana: State University Press.

Jeeves, M., ed. 2011. *Rethinking human nature: A multidisciplinary approach.* Grand Rapids, MI: Wm. B. Eerdmans Publishing Co.

Kilpatrick, W. 1985. *The Emperor's New Clothes: The naked truth about the new psychology.* Westchester, IL.: Crossway Books.

Knight, G. 2006. *Philosophy and Education: An introduction in Christian perspective, 4th Ed.* Berrien Springs, MI: Andrews University Press.

Laska, J. 1976. *Schooling and education: basic concepts and problems.* New York: Van Nostrand.

Learner-centered psychological principles: A framework for school reform and redesign. 1997. Washington, DC: American Psychological Association. (Derived from a 1990 APA presidential task force). Retrieved from http://www.apa.org/ed/governance/bea/learner-centered.pdf

LeBar, L. 1958. *Education that is Christian.* Old Tappan, New Jersey: Fleming H. Revell Company.

Lewis, C. S. 2010. "Christian Apologetics." *C.S. Lewis Essay Collection: Faith, Christianity and the Church.* L. Walmsley (Ed.). London: HarperCollins.

Lockerbie, D. B. 1981. *Who educates your child?: A book for parents.* Grand Rapids, MI: Zondervan Publishing House.

Long, J. & V. Frye. 1985. *Making it till Friday.* Princeton, NJ: Princeton Book Company Publishers.

MacCullough, M. 2012. *Developing a worldview approach to biblical integration, 4th ed.* Langhorne, PA: Cairn University.

MacLaine, S. 1985. *Dancing in the light.* New York, NY: Bantam Books.

McCallum, D. 1986. *The death of truth: What's wrong with multiculturalism, the rejection of reason and the new postmodern diversity.* Minneapolis, MN: Bethany House Publishers.

Milton, J. 1909–14. "Tractate on Education. *The Harvard Classics* (Vol. 3). New York, NY: Collier.

Moreland, J. P. 1997. *Love your God with all your mind: The role of reason in the life of the soul.* Colorado Springs, CO: NavPress.

Neill, A. S. 1960. *Summerhill: A radical approach to education.* New York: Hart.

Nicholi, A. M., Jr. 2002. *The question of God: C. S. Lewis and Sigmund Freud Debate God, Love, Sex, and the Meaning of Life.* New York, NY: Free Press, Simon and Schuster.

Plantinga, C., Jr. 2002. *Engaging God's world: A Christian vision of faith, learning, and living.* Grand Rapids, MI: Eerdmans Publishing Company.

Postman, N. 1996. *The end of education: Redefining the value of school.* New York, NY. Random House.

Rusk, R. R. 1956. *The philosophical bases of education, 2nd Ed.* Boston, MA: Houghton Mifflin.

Sartre, J. P. 1996. *Existential Psychoanalysis*. (H. E. Barnes, Trans.) Washington D.C.: Regnery Publishing, Inc.

Sire, J. W. 2004. *Naming the elephant: Worldview as a concept*. Downer's Grove, IL: InterVarsity Press.

Sire, J. W. 2009. *The universe next door, 5th ed*. Downer's Grove, IL: InterVarsity Press.

Slattery, P. 2006. *Curriculum development in the Postmodern era, 2nd Ed*. New York, NY: Routledge.

Social Science Staff of the Educational Research Council of America. 1971. The Human Adventure: Four World Views. Boston, MA: Allyn & Bacon.

Spears, P. & S. Loomis. 2009. *Educating for human flourishing: A Christian perspective*. Downer's Grove, IL: IVP Academic, InterVarsity Press

Spencer, H. 1860. *Education: intellectual, moral and physical*. New York, NY: D. Appleton & Company.

Steinem, G. 1992. *Revolution from within: A book of self-esteem*. United States of America: Gloria Steinem.

Sumner, W. G. 1911. *Folkways: A study of the sociological importance of usages, manners, customs, mores, and morals*. Boston, MA: Ginn and Co.

United Nations General Assembly. 1959. "Declaration of the Rights of the Child." Proclaimed by General Assembly Resolution 1386 (XIV) of 20 November 1959. PDF. Retrieved from http://www.unicef.org/lac/spbarbados/Legal/global/General/declaration_child1959.pdf

US Legal, Inc. 2012. Moral Authority Law and Legal Definition. Retrieved from http://definitions.uslegal.com/m/moral-authority

Von Glasersfeld, E. 1995. *Radical constructivism: a way of knowing and learning*. Washington, D.C.: The Falmer Press.

White, J. E. 2006. *A mind for God*. Downers Grove, IL: InterVarsity Press.

Woychuk, N. A. 1962. *God's glory displayed: Devotional exposition of 2 Corinthians 4:1–18*. Chicago: Moody Press.

Wright, N. T. 1992. *The New Testament and the People of God, Vol 1*. Minneapolis, MN: Augsburg Fortress Press.

Zacharias, R. 1997. *Deliver us from evil: Restoring the soul in a disintegrating culture*. Nashville, TN: W Publishing Group.

Zahorik, J. A. 1995. *Constructivist Teaching*. Bloomington, IN: Phi Delta Kappa Educational Foundation.

About the Author

Martha E. MacCullough is the Distinguished Professor Emerita in the Center for University Studies at Cairn University. She teaches at the undergraduate and graduate levels, as well as in Cairn's international graduate education programs in Europe, South America, and Asia. Formerly dean of the School of Education, Dr. MacCullough specializes in learning theory and learning methodology, philosophy of education, and biblical worldview integration.

Dr. MacCullough earned a doctorate of education degree from Temple University, a master of arts degree in Christian education from Wheaton College, and a bachelor of science in Bible degree with an international specialization from Cairn University.

Dr. MacCullough is, first and foremost, a teacher. However, she has also initiated and developed teacher education programs at two colleges. She was an administrator at Cairn for more than 30 years, during which time she developed 12 accredited teacher and educational leadership certification programs. In addition, TESOL (Teaching English to Speakers of Other Languages) and international education programs were developed under her supervision and are offered at the undergraduate and graduate levels on Cairn's main campus and on its international campuses in Europe, Asia, and South America. Her writing on educational issues such as human learning and worldview integration have been published in education books and journals and have been translated into several languages.

In addition to her teaching and responsibilities for the university, Dr. MacCullough conducts workshops at Christian education and teacher education conventions and conferences at the regional, national and international levels. She also conducts seminars on a variety of topics.